'Teach us delight in simple things.'
Rudyard Kipling

PLAIN

TERENCE CONRAN

SIMPLE

THE ESSENCE OF CONRAN STYLE

USEFUL

 conran OCTOPUS

To Vicki
Not plain, certainly not simple,
but very useful at times.

PLAIN

SIMPLE

USEFUL

----

introduction

introduction

The pace of modern life, with all its jolting distractions, increasingly means that the home must provide a solid, restorative framework for everyday life. First and foremost, that means it must serve the activities that take place within its walls. But, equally importantly, it must allow us to be ourselves, explore our tastes and feel comfortable in the broadest sense of the term.

I have always believed that objects – and surroundings – that are plain, simple and useful are the key to easy living. By grounding us in reality and performing well over time, they are as much the antidote to pointless complexity and superficial styling as they are to the shoddy and second-rate. Applied to the home as a whole, this discerning approach results in interiors that are effortlessly stylish, confident and timeless. In such surroundings, colour sings out, pattern adds verve and there is plenty of room for the expression of personal taste.

PLAIN

Plain means materials that speak for themselves, uncluttered form, and an absence of the kind of decoration that is designed to obscure rather than enhance.

SIMPLE

Simple implies both ease of operation and a direct connection with the type of elemental pleasures that we go away on holiday (vacation) to experience – the sun streaming through the windows, for example, the texture of a rug underfoot, or basic peace and quiet.

USEFUL

Useful means true practicality, rather than gadgets and appliances whose plethora of functions invent problems to solve. Equally, it is a chair that is the right height and a bed that provides the optimum degree of support.

Below — One of my most treasured possessions – and something that perfectly encapsulates the essence of 'plain, simple, useful' – is this bespoke cabinet of hand tools, which was a birthday present from Benchmark, our woodworking company.

I have often thought that people sometimes fight shy of this pared-back approach because they imagine it implies that they don't have enough money to spend. While it is true that simplicity can be economical – which is an advantage in itself – it is far from rough and ready, and sometimes not all that cheap. You only have to look at the designs of the Shakers to understand that plain, simple and useful things can often display a high degree of finesse and a superb handling of materials.

I was lucky enough to go to a school called Bryanston in Dorset (although my parents had to sell the family silver to pay the fees), where I was taught craftsmanship in metal, wood, stone and ceramics by a wonderful man called Don Potter, who had been a pupil of the typeface designer Eric Gill. I was also fortunate to be taught art by Charles Handley-Read.

What made an equally great impression on me, however, were the visits we made to stately homes near Blandford. Here we saw houses of amazing grandeur and sumptuous decoration, gilt and velvet everywhere, with walls covered in family portraits proclaiming that these rich families had well and truly arrived.

Somehow I always felt vaguely embarrassed by this brazen demonstration of so-called superiority and found myself wanting to look at the working parts of the house. I would wander off to the servants' quarters, where I was invariably delighted by the plain, simple and useful atmosphere of 'below stairs'. The wonderful kitchens where everything worked; the staff dining rooms with beautiful, rugged furnishings; the wine cellars, elegantly detailed; the dairies and gardeners' rooms full of practical things, fit for the job at hand.

This is what inspired me to become a designer of plain, simple and useful products and to reject the complexity of overdecoration and bling, the prime purpose of which is to show off success, wealth and status – what the *Financial Times* has recently identified as 'banker's style'. While I would readily admit that many intelligent and beautifully made things are expensive, I hope people might realize that a simple life is an easier one and, in the end, much more luxurious. For me, the perfect example of this entire approach is my cabinet of woodworking tools, a cherished birthday present from Benchmark, our bespoke woodworking company based at my home in the country.

THE WHOLE PICTURE

Sorting out the basics is half the battle. The infrastructure of servicing and the patterns of circulation must be right for your home to function as a whole and to work properly on every level. That means, among other things, installing enough radiators and power points and ensuring they are in the right places.

Pay attention to material character

○

Choose natural, solid surfaces and finishes that have the potential to wear well and improve with age. Don't tackle rooms on a piecemeal basis; instead, work out a limited palette of colours and textures, as expressed in the materials you select, and repeat them from area to area, as appropriate, to give a feeling of unity to your home.

Detailing is key

○

Well-designed and well-made details, such as handles, catches, taps (faucets), switches and power points, along with architectural features, such as door frames and skirting boards (baseboards), spell out a message of quality on an almost subconscious level – all the more so when touch is involved. When we redecorated our house in the country, we changed all the china door handles to nickel ones and the result was instantly fresher and more modern.

Making connections

○

We don't experience our homes in a static way, from only one viewpoint. During the course of a day we move from area to area, up and down stairs, and in and out of the front door. All these transitional spaces are just as important as the rooms where we spend more time. Routes need to be planned so that the different areas of the home connect in the most logical way; they also need to be kept clean and uncluttered so you have a sense of breathing space.

PLAIN

SIMPLE

USEFUL

----

cooking

Left — Glossy, reflective
surfaces and finishes make
the most of natural light.
The kitchen in our London
mews house has a glass
splashback and Corian
countertop. Downlights
recessed into the underside
of the shelf highlight the sink
below (see also pages 46–7).

cooking

When the kitchen first emerged from its 'below stairs' obscurity
in the immediate post-war years, the emphasis fell squarely on
labour-saving efficiency: surfaces and finishes that were easy
to keep clean and new appliances that took the drudgery out of
housework. Since then, the kitchen has variously morphed into
style statement, status symbol and domestic trophy – and it is fair
to say that many of these incarnations have been a great deal more
decorated and complicated than they needed to be. I am always
reminded of the *Masterchef* contestant who used a food processor
to chop a handful of walnuts, when a sharp knife would have done
the trick in a fraction of the time. Overelaborate 'professional'-style
kitchens that provide house room for every conceivable gadget
reveal the same misguided thinking. You don't need to spend a
fortune to create a kitchen that works well. In fact, a tight budget
can be a useful restraint, enabling you to focus on what really
matters. Cooking is a form of creativity that is accessible to all, so
the best kitchens are those that promote a hands-on approach.

Left — L-shaped layouts are very versatile and work equally well where space is limited as they do in kitchens that are more generously scaled. They are also ideal for open-plan living areas, as the working area of the kitchen is discreetly arranged in the background. Here the countertop and bar unit are in walnut.

Below — Island kitchens require much more floor space than other types of layout. The central island can house a sink and stovetop or simply serve as an additional food-preparation area. The raised height of the work surface makes routine tasks such as chopping more comfortable to perform while standing up.

Overleaf — With the working area of the kitchen along the length of one wall – an 'in-line' layout – there is space to include a generous dining table, here accompanied by a hospitable collection of mismatching chairs.

LAYOUTS

Kitchens that are efficient, comfortable and safe to work in have one thing in common: their layouts are based on the 'work triangle', a concept that dictates the optimum relationship between the three principal areas of activity.

○ Single-line, or in-line, layouts are best for open-plan spaces, narrow areas or where you need to conceal the kitchen for part of the time. You will need at least 3m (10ft) of wall space, with the longest stretch of worktop between the oven and the sink.

○ L-shaped kitchen layouts, which make use of two adjacent walls or a wall and a peninsula, work well in open-plan living/dining areas.

Use a carousel unit in the right-angle to maximize storage and avoid dead space.

○ Galley layouts arrange kitchen fixtures and fittings on facing walls, which should be no less than 1.2m (4ft) apart. These layouts are the best option where space is really tight.

○ U-shaped kitchen layouts, which make use of three walls or two walls and a peninsula, provide maximum storage and preparation space.

There should be at least 2m (6½ft) between the arms of the 'U' for optimum efficiency and ease of use.

○ Island layouts, where the kitchen is arranged around a central island for cooking, food preparation and/or storage, require more floor area than other kitchen configurations.

Left — For many years, the kitchen at our house in the country has been the centre of our family life and now welcomes a new generation of grandchildren.

The long, rectangular dining table is placed at right angles to the island unit, while an array of copper pans and a batterie de cuisine make eye-catching displays.

Below — The working area of this open-plan kitchen is bathed in natural light from above, while the glazed end wall merges the dining area with the terrace outside.

Overleaf — This family kitchen has a great sense of inclusiveness thanks to the open layout, which preserves connections between indoors and out, and between eating

and living areas. In the kitchen, floorboards give way to more practical flooring, but since the two materials are tonally similar, the shift is less obtrusive.

FAMILY KITCHENS

Generous, inclusive in spirit and supporting an assortment of different activities aside from cooking and preparing food, family kitchens more than merit their status as the living, beating heart of the home. But when the kitchen functions as occasional admin centre, playroom, dining area and unofficial living room, how do you keep chaos – visual and otherwise – at bay?

One answer is to plan the cooking area very tightly, while providing some degree of separation – counter, shelf units or sliding doors – to screen it from the rest of the space. Good organization is also key. Whatever drifts into the kitchen, simply because it is the main place where people gather, either should be routinely returned to its proper place or given a dedicated storage area of its own away from the

food-preparation area. This applies to bills and paperwork as much as it does to toys, homework and art supplies.

Keep an eye on safety issues and maintenance. Avoid trailing wires and fit childproof locks to cabinets where cleaning products are stored. Choose surfaces and finishes that are easy to keep clean. A portion of wall painted with blackboard paint makes a useful household message board.

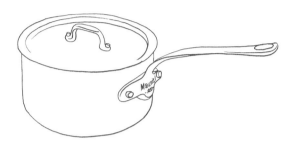

MAUVIEL
COPPER COOKWARE

Serious cooks swear by their copper pans and for good reason. Copper is an excellent conductor of heat, eight times more efficient than stainless steel and one and a half times more efficient than aluminium. Equally important, copper conducts heat evenly. Pans made of less conductive materials tend to have hot spots where food can stick and burn. Copper pans are highly reactive to temperature changes, which makes them ideal for many different types of cooking, most particularly sautéing, casseroling, and making sauces and pastry.

Mauviel, a French family-run firm based in Villedieu-les-Poêles, Normandy – the 'city of copper' – has been making classic copper cookware since 1830. Today the company produces more than 1,000 different pots and pans, from *bains-maries* to cocottes and fondue sets, in a range of materials including stainless steel and aluminium as well as copper. Their M'héritage range is 90 per cent copper on the outside with a 10 per cent stainless-steel lining, to facilitate cleaning, and varnished cast-iron handles.

Copper cookware is undoubtedly both expensive and more demanding to maintain, but, in addition to gleaming good looks, you also get a lifetime's worth of service and a high degree of control.

Below — Occupying a corner under the slope of the eaves, this compact kitchen is so simply laid out it can be understood at a glance. The vivid unit fronts provide a welcome dash of colour.

Right — Small kitchens tend to be one-person operations, and galley layouts are ideal for the purpose. Here, the pale-toned, wide floorboards enhance the sense of space and lead the eye onwards.

SMALL KITCHENS

Small kitchens, as many professional chefs could tell you, can be highly efficient and creative places. On the domestic front, a compact kitchen is probably going to be a one-person operation, so ensure that the layout feels natural to you – or to whoever is going to be doing the cooking.

To make the most of limited space, opt for a fully fitted layout and spend enough time at the planning stage to come up with the optimum arrangement. Extend the same thinking to the interiors of drawers and cupboards, customizing them if necessary with dividers, baskets and adjustable shelves so that no space is wasted. Pull-out or fold-down flaps can usefully extend worktops or serve as a breakfast counter.

When it comes to equipment, focus on a hardworking basic collection of kit – this is not the place for specialist appliances or utensils, unless they are in regular use. The same is true of provisions.

Light, bright and reflective surfaces and finishes are naturally space-enhancing. Flush panels and drawer fronts keep visual distraction to a minimum. Another strategy to make the room look bigger is to remove the plinth from the base of built-in units so that the floor is uninterrupted.

Left — This high-ceilinged
room with its original
cornicing has been fitted
out with a combination of
open shelving, clean-lined
contemporary kitchen
units and more traditional

glass-fronted cabinetry –
painted the same colour for
unification – creating a highly
effective blend of old and new.

Below — Wood cladding
adds depth of character to a
streamlined, well-integrated
layout. The warmth of the
ceiling finish especially helps
to counteract the expanse of
polished concrete flooring.

FITTED KITCHENS

Ever popular since the 1950s, the fitted
kitchen suits all types of layout and is by
far the best option if you have limited
space or if you need to include a kitchen
within an open-plan area. Produced
in modular sizes to conform with
standard appliance dimensions, fitted
units allow you to integrate the three
main cooking zones with great visual
neatness and practical efficiency.

Whether mass-market designs in
largely synthetic materials, bespoke
cabinetry in solid wood or professional
units in steel and glass, their price and
style will vary widely. Whatever your
budget, look out for clean lines,
unobtrusive catches and handles, and
neat detailing – avoid fussy fielded
panelling or countrified decoration.
If you have inherited a fitted kitchen
that is looking a little tired, an economic
way of giving it a facelift is to change the
drawer and unit fronts.

Even at the lower end of the market,
a fitted kitchen is still a substantial
investment – and, once installed, it is
not easy to change. Plan carefully, with
the aid of an in-store service if possible,
to ensure that you make the most of
available space.

Left — Freestanding drawer
units and a central island
reminiscent of a traditional
butcher's block update
the unfitted kitchen for the
twenty-first century.

Below — An industrial-style
stainless-steel freestanding
storage unit, along with
built-in cabinets raised
on legs, give this kitchen
a professional edge.

UNFITTED KITCHENS

Most kitchens contain at least some
freestanding elements, but few are
entirely unfitted – the fixed points
of servicing see to that. You have
to go some way back in time – to
the prewar below-stairs domain of
domestic servants – to find kitchens
that were composed exclusively of
separate elements.

The most common unfitted elements
to be found in contemporary kitchens
are large appliances, such as
freestanding refrigerators and
range-style cookers. Even so, these
are not usually stranded in space, but
anchored within a fitted framework.

Traditional freestanding pieces of
kitchen furniture – the Welsh dresser
(hutch) or butcher's block table, for
example – can be a little self-consciously
nostalgic in a contemporary home,
although modern reinterpretations
of these classic designs can display
a pleasing simplicity and integrity
of material. Mid-century modern
cabinets and reclaimed shop fittings
have a retro appeal.

A modern variation on the same idea
is those modular units where sinks and
even stoves are integrated within
a freestanding housing – similar to a
workbench – ready to be connected
to existing servicing. The principal
advantages of such pieces is that they
allow for flexible arrangement and
represent a portable investment.

LIGHTING

Good kitchen lighting promotes safety and efficiency first and foremost. But you will also need to build in a degree of flexibility, with dimmers, for example, to accommodate the social side of things.

○ Kitchens need light levels that are up to three times higher than those required for living areas. Watch out for glare off reflective surfaces, however, as this may dazzle you and pose a danger when you are working with hot pans and sharp knives. Lighting should be bright but even.

○ Floor lamps and table lamps can provide ambient light for eating areas but avoid them in the kitchen itself, where trailing wires are a hazard.

○ For general background lighting, wall-mounted uplights are very effective. Pendants hung low over the table provide a welcoming focus for eating areas within kitchens; a line of pendants is also an attractive and practical way to light a worktop.

Left — A charming ad hoc arrangement of frosted bulbs suspended at different heights from a steel rail provides glare-free task lighting over a kitchen counter.

Below — Recessed downlights are carefully positioned over the island worktop and preparation areas, while the glazed end wall bathes the eating area in natural light. Pale-toned reflective surfaces and finishes further enhance the airy, spacious effect.

○ Target task light at preparation areas so you are not working in your own shadow. Directional spotlights, tracklights and adjustable downlights are all practical options.

○ Striplights mounted on the underside of wall-hung units or concealed behind baffles illuminate worktops evenly and without glare.

○ Dimmers allow you to lower light levels when you sit down to eat and are no longer busy at the stove.

Left — A combination of different materials – shiny laminate unit fronts, wood flooring and stone worktop – work effortlessly together because they share the same muted palette.

SURFACES AND FINISHES

Like bathrooms, kitchens demand surfaces and finishes that are waterproof and easy to maintain. Heat- and stain-resistance are also considerations for worktops and splashbacks; flooring that is relatively nonslip is advisable.

While plain, simple and useful means choosing materials that are fit for purpose, it also means selecting those that repay any effort in upkeep with continued good looks. Cheap artificial materials – thin laminates, poor-quality vinyl and such like – have little wear-resistance and will need to be replaced sooner rather than later. Solid natural materials, on the other hand, improve with use if they are cared for and maintained correctly, even though they cost more at the outset. A further advantage is that their depth of character and textural interest more than compensate for the muted palette of colours that they display.

Pay special attention to the junctions where one material abuts another. Wherever possible, opt for a single continuous surface, or at least keep joints to a minimum, to promote a seamless look. This is not only visually neat but also more hygienic. Many worktops can be produced with integral sinks and splashbacks.

Wood

While wooden surfaces are often associated with the rustic or country kitchen, they can also have a sleek contemporary look. Oiled hardwood worktops, smooth wood-veneer cladding for cupboards and counters, and polished solid or veneered hardwood floors are good-looking and practical, provided that you seal them against moisture penetration and staining.

The most water-resistant wood floor of all is engineered oak, which is a laminate comprising a thick veneer over a cross veneer, with another layer at the bottom. I should know: it is the flooring in our bathroom and when I overflowed the tub the other day, not a drop penetrated the library ceiling below.

Stone

A classic choice for kitchens, stone conveys a certain timeless quality. Most types must be sealed; marble, in particular, stains easily. Options for flooring include slate, limestone, sandstone and granite, with the honed or riven finishes providing more grip underfoot. Polished granite worktops are pleasingly flecked and come in a variety of colours.

Tile

Ceramic tile is the workhorse of fitted areas, such as kitchens and bathrooms. Metro-style formats or mosaic for splashbacks offer more visual interest than standard dimensions. Tiling is a good way of delivering colour, although tiles that are busily patterned may be a little too intrusive, particularly if they extend over large areas. Be generous with tiled surfaces – a small margin around working areas looks skimpy. Unless you have real expertise, always have the work professionally done – the grid of tiling makes any unevenness all too visible.

Below — A wall of built-in units faced in gleaming stainless steel makes a sleek contemporary backdrop in a minimally detailed kitchen/eating area.

Below right — White metro tiling extending over the entire wall, together with a herringbone parquet hardwood floor, have a retro appeal.

Glass

As a worktop or splashback, glass is unobtrusive, clean-lined and relatively easy to maintain. Backlit glass panels introduce light and colour in a subtle way. Glass-fronted wall units, frosted or clear, keep contents visible and dust-free, and are lighter in appearance than those with solid doors.

Stainless steel

No-nonsense stainless-steel finishes – for work surfaces, splashbacks or unit fronts – have a professional edge. Unrelieved expanses of steel can be a little cold and forbidding, however. Stainless steel also has a tendency to mark and maintenance can be demanding.

Composites and laminates

There is a wide variety of artificial materials available for kitchen use, from laminates made of bonded layers of paper to composites manufactured from resins, some of which can be individually specified. Cheap laminates are a false economy: look for up-market versions. Most synthetic surfaces are easy to wipe down and keep clean; few, however, are heatproof and none age particularly well.

Below — A composite worktop with integral trim features an inset sink, combining neatness with good looks.

Below right — Polished concrete has a certain monumental quality. Bespoke features, such as this counter, are generally cast in situ.

Overleaf — The working area of our mews kitchen is screened from the staircase by a toughened glass panel. It is separated from the main eating area by an oak unit that is staggered in height to form a breakfast bar on one side and a preparation area on the other. The side of the counter is clad with polished pewter to visually reduce its bulk.

Concrete

As a flooring or worktop, concrete has a basic simplicity. Polished concrete surfaces are less brutal than the more textured finishes.

Linoleum and vinyl

Available in either tile or sheet format, lino and vinyl are popular kitchen floor coverings. Yet whereas vinyl is wholly artificial and often looks it, lino is a natural product that improves with age. Hygienic, warm and stain-resistant, it comes in a variety of subtle mottled colours.

Paint

One of the easiest ways of introducing colour into the kitchen is through painted surfaces. Oil-based paint, such as eggshell, which can be wiped down, is more practical than water-based emulsion (latex), which may show spattering. Moisture-resistant paints designed specifically for kitchens and bathrooms are also available.

FOOD STORAGE

One of the great challenges of kitchen
organization is ensuring that a wide
variety of different foodstuffs, all with
their own optimum keeping conditions,
are stored as efficiently and accessibly
as possible.

○ Store basic condiments that are in
daily use near the food-preparation
area, so they are readily to hand.

○ Spices are best kept away from heat
and light. An array of narrow shelves
the depth of a typical spice jar allow you
to select the right ingredient at a glance.

○ Decant bulk packages of dried food
– rice, pasta, pulses and grains – into
sealed and labelled storage jars to
prevent spillage and spoilage.

○ Refrigeration is not the only storage
solution for fresh food. A larder can be
better for those types of food that need
to remain cool but not so chilled that
their flavour is impaired.

○ Pull-out wicker baskets and wire
racks keep root vegetables well aerated.

○ Don't overfill your refrigerator or
you will compromise its efficiency.

○ Large chest or freestanding freezers
only make sense if you cook in bulk
or need to store supplies over a long
period. A decent-sized freezer
compartment is usually sufficient.

○ Wine storage is an art in itself.
Wines for regular consumption are
best racked on their sides in a cool,
dark, dry location.

KILNER

JAR

Before reliable refrigeration became available to ordinary householders, food preservation by pickling, salting or preserving was essential to supplement the diet throughout the lean winter months. Nowadays, these methods may play less essential roles in our daily lives but, as home enthusiasts can testify, there is something deeply satisfying about making thrifty use of surplus fruit and vegetables from the kitchen garden or allotment.

The Kilner jar, a classic larder standby and time-honoured feature of the well-stocked kitchen store cupboard, dates back to 1842. The design was the brainchild of John Kilner, an Englishman, and was subsequently manufactured in large numbers by his Yorkshire firm. The original preserving jar was produced with a glass plug and rubber seal. More recent versions feature rubberized metal screw tops or clip tops with seals.

The Kilner jar has inspired many imitations. Similar patented examples are the Mason or Ball jar, an American design first introduced in 1858, and the French Le Parfait jars, which have been in use for more than 70 years. Such jars are equally useful as airtight storage canisters for many other foodstuffs aside from preserves.

Below — The self-contained larder, preferably one that is naturally cooled and ventilated, provides ideal keeping conditions for a variety of different foodstuffs and bulk supplies.

Right — A pantry cupboard with integral lighting features narrow spice racks mounted onto the backs of the double doors, along with neatly organized storage for wine, bread, dried goods and preserves. There is even enough room to stow additional items such as a collection of coffee pots and a food processor.

LARDERS

Modern households are hugely dependent on the refrigerator for food storage, almost by default. Consequently, refrigerators have grown ever larger in size until they are now quite a dominant feature in many kitchens. While reliable refrigeration has undoubtedly been a boon, the cool environment of a traditional larder offers better keeping conditions for foods such as fruit and vegetables, cheese, ham, salami, game and preserves, all of which need to mature to develop their full flavour.

In times past, the larder was sited on the side of the house that faced away from the sun and had at least two (preferably three) external well-ventilated walls. The natural cooling was further enhanced by a stone or tiled floor and stone (often slate) shelving. If you don't have a suitable space to fit out as a larder, an alternative would be to include a pantry cupboard in your kitchen. These are typically tall freestanding or built-in units with shelves of varying heights and depths, pull-out baskets and racks. While they may lack the natural cooling properties of the true larder, you can at least plan the layout so that the pantry cupboard is sited away from the stove and other heat sources and preferably against a cool external wall.

BASIC EQUIPMENT

You don't need to spend a fortune on specialist equipment to produce good food. An appliance that takes longer to clean and reassemble than it does to operate, or one that you use so rarely that you need consult the manual before you even switch it on, are often more trouble than they are worth. More to the point, they are occupying valuable space that could be better used to store something else. From bread-makers to grapefruit knives, any item of specialist kit, no matter how beguiling, must be in regular use to warrant house room.

Where you should not skimp is on quality. Decent knives, well-made pots and pans, and robust everyday utensils – spoons, mixing bowls, colanders, sieves (strainers), corkscrews and such like – will always repay investment and, with the right care and maintenance, have the potential to last a lifetime.

The same approach should be adopted when you are choosing large appliances. Buy the best quality you can afford and pay particular attention to build quality. A retro-styled refrigerator in a quirky colour may lift your spirits, but ensure that it is robust enough to deliver reliable performance, as this is going to matter more on a daily basis.

Left — A good rule of thumb for kitchen display: whatever you place out on view should be in regular use, whether this is glassware, china, pans, serving dishes or cookery

books. This kitchen demonstrates a workable and practical balance between open shelving and concealed storage.

Below — Accents of colour and intriguing textural contrasts can be supplied by the simplest of means: a plate of lemons, vivid tumblers, chopping boards

and ceramics; all pieces from our exclusive homeware collection for M&S.

KITCHEN DISPLAYS

While kitchens are naturally cheery and hospitable places, they are also hardworking. This does not rule out decorative display but it does suggest that most of what you leave out on view should largely relate in some way to the main focus of activity – platters of fresh fruit and vegetables, for example, fresh herbs growing in pots or foodstuffs in intriguing packaging.

Aside from framed prints, posters or artwork, which are as welcome in the kitchen as they are anywhere else, whatever you display should ideally be used on a regular basis. Even the most efficiently ventilated kitchen attracts grease and dust. Colourful dishes, jugs (pitchers) or enamelled cookware can contribute a lively visual interest arranged on opening shelving, but if they are only pressed into service once in a blue moon, you have unnecessarily added the chore of cleaning them first to your list of things to do.

One of the most appealing of all kitchen displays is the batterie de cuisine, suspended from a metal rail or rack. En masse, a grouping of slotted spoons, whisks, colanders, polished copper pans and other basic utensils has a pleasing sculptural quality.

MOKA
ESPRESSO POT

Familiar to generations of coffee enthusiasts around the world, the Moka espresso pot has been manufactured by the Italian firm Bialetti since 1933. The design, patented by Luigi De Ponti and developed by the firm's founder, Alfonso Bialetti (1888–1970), represented the first affordable means of making espresso at home. Initially sold in local markets, it is now estimated that 90 per cent of Italian households own at least one.

Made of aluminium with a Bakelite handle, the eight-sided stovetop pot uses steam pressure to brew the coffee. The lower section holds the water, a central filter contains the ground coffee, and the top of the pot is where the brewed coffee collects. It comes in a range of sizes.

After the Second World War an advertising campaign brought the Moka pot to wider attention. A key element of the promotion was the Bialetti mascot, designed by the artist Paul Campani in 1953. The 'little man with a moustache' that features on the side of the pot was intended to distinguish the Moka pot from other, similar designs coming onto the market at this time.

PLAIN

SIMPLE

USEFUL

----

eating

eating

In many homes today, eating is a movable feast. From the snatched breakfast at the kitchen counter to the sit-down Sunday lunch with family and friends that goes on all afternoon, mealtimes are far from being as structured or as formal as they once were. And if times are not fixed, neither are locations. This is reflected in the gradual disappearance of the separate dining room, which has increasingly been absorbed into other multipurpose spaces.

Sharing a meal together on a regular basis creates an important bond and fosters communication. It is social glue – unlike eating off a tray in front of the television or grazing throughout the day. So it is worth making the effort to create a hospitable eating area, even if it is located within an open-plan layout. Here psychological breathing space is just as important as the physical sort.

If you don't have much room at your disposal, you will need to build a degree of flexibility into your arrangements when it comes to entertaining. Extendable tables and stackable or foldable extra chairs are practical ways of accommodating guests.

Left — You need plenty of floor area if you are going to site a dining table right at the heart of things. It is also best to opt for an in-line layout that arranges the kitchen along the length of a wall (see page 25).

Below — A peninsula clad in wood veneer screens off the working part of the kitchen and makes a sympathetic backdrop to the eating area. The Wishbone chairs are by Hans Wegner (see page 73).

Bottom — Cooking and eating are natural partners. Here a galley layout (see page 25) with concealed built-in appliances leads to a dining table positioned only a few steps away from the stove.

All the kitchen surfaces are made of Corian, which is both practical and pleasant to touch. The bar stools are flea-market finds, while the cherry wood dining table was designed by Anders Heger.

EATING IN THE KITCHEN

Sitting down to eat where food has been prepared and cooked makes perfect sense: there is something appealingly immediate about meals served direct from oven to table. At the same time, the enjoyment of food and company seems natural within a space that often serves as the focal point of the entire household.

Yet however much cooking and eating are related, the two activities need to be separated in some way. So far as cooking is concerned, you don't want to be distracted when you are handling hot pans or sharp knives or juggling timings. Plenty of cooks, even the most confident, find it difficult to concentrate when their every move is on view. By the same token, kitchen surfaces that look like a bombsite don't make an appetizing background for a relaxing, enjoyable meal.

LE CREUSET

CASSEROLE

Nothing epitomizes the robust good looks of oven-to-tableware more than Le Creuset. Made of enamelled cast iron, the classic Volcanic range dates back to 1925. Weighty, exceptionally durable, ideal for stewing and other forms of slow cooking, the design looks as stylish on the tabletop as it does on the stovetop or in the oven. Handles and lid knobs may be integral cast iron or black phenolic resin.

Le Creuset was founded by Armand Desaegher, who was a specialist in casting, and Octave Aubecq, whose expertise was enamelling. The company is based in Fresnoy-le-Grand, Picardy, France, where its cast-iron products are still made. The Volcanic casserole showed off the founders' ability to add pigment to enamel, and the familiar iconic orange shade was chosen to echo the molten interior of a cauldron. Nowadays, the casseroles are available in different shapes, sizes and colours, including off-white.

The cookware is manufactured using standard casting methods. Subsequent finishing work, however, is still largely hand-done before the pots are sprayed with two coats of enamel.

LAYOUT IN DINING AREAS

In a kitchen/dining area, the easiest way to distinguish one activity from the other is through layout. Either that can arise naturally from the disposition of the space itself, or you can give it a helping hand with the furniture arrangement or the way fitted units are planned and installed.

○ Unless your kitchen is exceptionally spacious, try to avoid siting a dining table right in the middle of the layout where it will necessarily disrupt routes to and from the main preparation and cooking areas.

○ Keep it consistent. The eating area should display the same overall style and approach as the kitchen itself.

○ Big, robust tables are ideal for family kitchens and will take the kind of punishment that small children routinely hand out. Between meals they can serve as a place for tackling homework or creative projects.

○ Space-saving ideas include fold-down or pull-out surfaces that double up as places to eat and extra preparation space.

○ Screen the working area of the kitchen from the eating area with a peninsula or counter to give the cook a little privacy.

○ Efficient ventilation is always important in a kitchen; all the more so if you are going to be eating there as well.

○ If you are seriously short of space, consider extending your kitchen a short way out into the garden, either to the side or to the rear, or both. Glazed extensions, especially those that can be opened onto the garden on fine days, make uplifting eating areas.

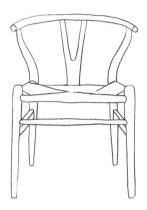

WISHBONE
CHAIR

Danish designer Hans Wegner (1914–2007) was one of the leading practitioners of the mid-century Scandinavian modern style. His Round chair, described by the American magazine *Interiors* as 'the world's most beautiful chair', was chosen as seating for the televised debates between John F Kennedy and Richard Nixon in 1960, helping to bring the work of Danish designers to an international audience.

Another iconic design, the Y or Wishbone chair (1949), epitomizes Wegner's approach: a mastery of form, an honesty of construction and an instinctive handling of material. Apprenticed to a carpenter, he never abandoned wood, and in a long and prolific career he produced more than 500 designs for chairs, continually exploring notions of simplicity and purity.

Like the Round chair, the Wishbone provides just the right degree of support for dining. Simple and elegant in form, the semicircular top rail and splayed support echo the curve of the back legs. Originally made in teak, the chair is now produced by Carl Hansen & Son in a variety of woods, including maple, ash, beech, oak, cherry and walnut. The seat is made of paper cord and the frame is machined from solid wood.

LIVING/DINING AREAS

Another natural pairing, the living/ dining area may be less immediate or family-oriented than the inclusive kitchen, but it can be every bit as welcoming. With food preparation going on elsewhere, there is no requirement to screen views of meals in progress. Similarly, it is often easier to generate a sense of occasion when you are entertaining.

In most homes, the distance between the kitchen and living/dining area is not considerable. Even so, try to ensure that the route between the two is as direct as possible to make serving and clearing away easier.

As with kitchen eating areas, it is important to arrange matters so there is a clear separation of activities. At the most prosaic, this may involve placing the dining table at one end of the space or, for example, in the 'foot' of an L-shaped room. Bay windows also provide a sense of enclosure that help differentiate eating areas from relaxing areas. Otherwise, think about furniture arrangement. Freestanding dividers – or even the back of a sofa – can signal the shift from one part of the room to another.

Left — Separate dining rooms are something of a luxury in today's homes. Furnished simply, however, they can successfully fulfil other roles between mealtimes.

Below — The Berger chair, with its webbed seat and back, and the Cairns bench and dining table in oak come from the homewares collection we have recently designed exclusively for the American retailer JCPenney. The bespoke pieces marry a clean-lined contemporary simplicity with what I like to call a dash of British charm.

Overleaf — Dramatic copper-lined glass pendants by Tom Dixon are hung over a pair of simple tables pushed together. The assortment of chairs includes a couple of Tripp Trapp children's chairs by Peter Opsvik from 1972, along with classic Eames DSR chairs (1950) and Arne Jacobsen Series 7 (model 3107) chairs (1955).

SEPARATE DINING ROOMS

A room dedicated solely to eating is fairly unusual these days. First, few households have the space for it and, second, its formality seems at odds with modern lifestyles. In older houses that have undergone conversion, where walls have come down, they have most often come down between dining rooms and adjacent areas.

While a separate dining room does not have to be a relic of the past, it is generally more successful as a space if it serves other purposes between mealtimes – as a study or a library, perhaps. This helps to maintain a sense of animation, which can otherwise be lacking. Similarly, if you are going to have a dedicated room set aside for eating, use it throughout the day and not just for the evening meal or when you are entertaining.

Furnishing and decoration can help to dispel any hint of starchy formality. Avoid heavy curtains and carpeting that can hold food odours and keep surfaces and finishes simple. Clean-lined contemporary dining furniture – glass-topped trestles, refectory-style tables, simple bentwood or leather-clad chairs and such like – lend itself to other uses between mealtimes.

Below — A wood-burning
stove supplies psychological
as well as physical warmth –
and is a welcome focal point
in an eating area.

Right — A collection of
black-and-white photographs
and prints casually propped
on narrow shelves gives the
eye something to linger on.

CREATING A FOCUS

The table – and the food you serve –
is rightly the focus of attention of any
mealtime. Whatever the shape of the
table – round, square, rectangular or
oval – ensure that there is enough room
around it for people to move their chairs
in and out comfortably.

You can enhance this psychological
breathing space further through
lighting. If possible, arrange things
so the table is set up near a window.
A good view, as much as natural
light, promotes an expansive feeling.
Pendants, particularly those with
glare-reducing louvred shades, draw
people together within the same
hospitable circle. Show-stopping
designs, such as contemporary takes
on the chandelier, also add glamour
and promote a sense of occasion.

In multipurpose spaces, a change
of flooring material goes a long way to
signal a shift from one area to the next.
In a kitchen/diner, for example, you
might consider tiling the working area
of the room and switching to a light
hardwood floor of a similar tone in the
eating area. A slight change in level –
a few steps up or down – works in a
similar way. Flatweave rugs placed
under the table can also help to
demarcate space.

Left — With its 72 overlapping leaves, Poul Henningsen's PH Artichoke pendant (1958) was designed to provide glare-free light from any direction. It has great sculptural presence. The

chairs are Arne Jacobsen's Series 7 (model 3107) designs.

Below — Pendant lights suspended over a dining table should not obscure the views of diners on opposite sides,

or be hung so low that you run the risk of bumping your head on them. This simple example features two frosted bulbs. The chairs are the DSR design by Eames and the Ant chair by Arne Jacobsen (1952).

Overleaf left — A collection of coloured Eames DSR chairs surrounds a dining table lit by a vintage Jacobsen glass pendant. The overscaled fork in the background is an amusing touch.

Overleaf right — The green industrial pendant, rustic wooden table and metal café chairs in front of this in-line kitchen have the timeless appeal and fresh simplicity of French country style.

LIGHTING

Nothing – aside from the food on your plate – enhances the experience of eating more than good lighting. Fast-food outlets are overbright because the driving force of such businesses is quick turnover. While you don't want to go to the opposite extreme and dine in sepulchral gloom, it is important to bear in mind that much lower levels of light are needed for eating than for cooking.

○ If you light the table with a pendant, make sure it hangs at the right height. Too low and you will restrict views across the table – and you may even hit your head, which I have seen often enough. Too high and you run the risk of creating glare because the light source will be visible.

○ Wall lights or modern sconces are good sources of general background illumination and have no trailing wires to create a hazard when you are moving around the table.

○ Adjustable spots and downlights can also be useful in eating areas, particularly if you target them to bounce light off walls, instead of aiming them directly at the table.

○ Dimmers are a must, especially for eating areas situated within kitchens.

○ A tablescape of candles in contemporary holders is instantly evocative; candlelight is flattering and creates an intimate atmosphere.

Left — The open-plan eating
area on the ground floor of
our mews house is furnished
with a plain black wooden
rectangular table and
graceful Thonet bentwood

chairs, one of my favourite
designs. The brightly painted
supporting girders provide
bold accents of colour and
bring a strong vertical
emphasis to the space.

Below — Shared mealtimes
are the heart of family life.
What is on the plate, not the
plate itself, should always
be the focus of attention.

TABLE SETTINGS

The table, these days, is far less 'dressed'
than those of our grandparents, when
the accoutrements of dining were many
and various and a place setting could
run to several different forks, knives
and spoons. While I am not about to
argue for a return to those days of fussy
starched napery and fish knives, there
is still a place for care and finesse when
it comes to setting the table. Well-
chosen cutlery (flatware) that feels good
in the hand, robust tumblers, stemmed
glasses for wine, and china that is
generously sized convey a thoughtful
attention to detail, without detracting
from the food.

Keeping it simple means using
oven-to-table serving dishes wherever
possible, but that does not mean a
rough-and-ready approach. Well-
designed casseroles, platters, soup
tureens and salad bowls contribute
a pleasing sculptural quality to the
table and are also a good means of
introducing accents of colour in limited
doses. Heavily patterned plates and
bowls, on the other hand, can argue
with the appetizing beauty of the food.

For special occasions, it is hard to
better the classic elegance of plain white
table linen. I believe that most of the
colour on the table should come from
what is on your plate, and white table
linen makes the perfect background
for any meal.

DURALEX
GLASSWARE

The glassware company Duralex, based in La Chapelle-Saint-Mesmin in north-central France, has been making toughened glass products for more than 80 years using their own proprietary tempering process, invented in 1939. Duralex tempered glass is two and a half times stronger than ordinary glass. The company is the only glassware manufacturer that makes all of its products in France.

The best-known of the Duralex range are the Picardie and Provence glasses, plain, functional tumblers that are both heat- and shatter-resistant. Because they are so durable and resist chipping, they have long been a familiar sight in cafés, brasseries and schools, but they are equally versatile in a domestic setting. They come in a variety of sizes, can be used for hot or cold drinks, are stackable to save storage space and are safe to use in the microwave, freezer and dishwasher. Most importantly, their contoured shapes feel comfortable in the hand and their inherent simplicity of form makes them at home on any table, whether you are serving water, juice, beer or lattes.

STORAGE

Storage furniture for eating areas has undergone a transformation over the years. Nowadays, low contemporary cabinets in metal or wood take the place of ponderous sideboards, and bulky dressers (hutches) have been reinterpreted as sleek versatile highboards with minimal detailing. Such unobtrusive solutions are particularly effective in living/eating areas because they lend themselves to multipurpose use and don't have 'dining room' written all over them. They can also double up as places for display.

If you are eating in the kitchen, on the other hand, storage is more likely to be built in, with china, glassware and cutlery (flatware) kept in fitted units along with basic foodstuffs and pots and pans. Group everything you need for the table – plates, mugs, glasses and cutlery (flatware) – in the same general location, preferably one that is easily accessible both from the dishwasher or sink and from the dining table. Glass-fronted wall units allow you to see what you have at a glance.

The plain, simple, useful approach suggests that rather than maintain two different sets of cutlery (flatware), glassware and dishes – one for everyday and one for 'best' – you select one good-quality set. This, in turn, will reduce the amount of space you have to give over to storage.

○ Open shelves of china and glassware have undoubted eye-appeal. Try to restrict such displays to items that you use on a regular basis.

○ When it comes to plates and dishes, store in small stacks no more than eight pieces high to help prevent chipping. Keep like with like – sizes, shapes, patterns, colours. Glasses should always be stored upright and arranged by type and size. Nest cups instead of suspending them from their handles.

○ Serving platters and catering-size dishes that you use only a few times a year can be stored remotely if you are short of space in the kitchen or eating area. The same applies to table linen that only comes out on special occasions.

○ Keep cutlery (flatware) in divided drawers or customize a standard drawer with an insert. If you have inherited silverware, this should be kept separately, preferably in velvet bags or a felt-lined container to reduce scratching and tarnishing.

○ Periodically spend some time reviewing what you own. Discard chipped or cracked plates, mugs and cups, which are no more hygienic than they are pleasing to the eye.

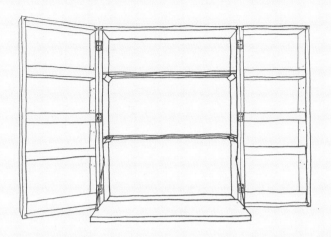

PROJECT #1

DRINKS CUPBOARD

I have always believed that the key to plain, simple and useful living is good organization, which entails both keeping a firm grip on possessions and providing enough dedicated storage space to house them efficiently. This drinks cupboard, the first of three projects I have specifically designed for this book, has been constructed by Benchmark, our bespoke woodworking firm based at my home in the country. For those of you who are confident of your DIY skills, full step-by-step instructions on how to make the cupboard can be viewed online at www.octopusbooks.co.uk/psu.

All three cupboards are variations on the same basic theme: a wall-hung cabinet with hinged doors. As with any storage unit, however, it is how the interior is arranged that makes all the difference. Here the hinged doors are fitted with a series of narrow shelves for storing glassware and small bottles and cans of mixers. The main body of the cabinet features two glass shelves, fixed far enough apart and of sufficient depth to take bottles of spirits and liqueurs – and are easy to wipe clean of spills. The fold-down panel makes a convenient surface where you can hone your bartending skills and whip up the perfect Bloody Mary or Dry Martini. A small bolt and lock could be added to keep the contents secure.

PLAIN

SIMPLE

USEFUL

---

relaxing

Left — Grey sectional seating
and small upholstered seats
in the living room of our
mews house provide a place
to relax near the open fire.

Overleaf — This loft-style
living room, with its exposed
brick walls, is furnished with
a number of pieces from our
exclusive homewares

collection for JCPenney,
which includes chairs,
tables, beds and sofas, as
well as lighting, textiles
and accessories.

relaxing

Relaxation takes many forms. For some, it is sitting quietly with a good book. For others, it is listening to loud music. In the case of young children, who at certain ages seem to lack an 'off' button, full-on, boisterous, energetic play is their version of unwinding.

If relaxing is hard to pin down, a related difficulty is coming up with a fixed purpose for living areas. In the past, the 'front room' was a public space, a place to entertain guests and show off your status. Paradoxically, this meant that in many households it was shut up for much of the time. Nowadays, unless you live alone (and sometimes even then), the living area, by default, is going to be multi-use to some extent. This means the challenge is to demarcate different areas of activity so that one does not overwhelm the others.

What all living areas should provide, however, is comfort, both the physical sort – chairs and sofas that support the body in repose – and the visual kind – welcoming levels of lighting, and objects and focal points for the eye to linger on.

Left — Comfort is a matter
of personal taste. Here an
Eames RAR rocker (1950)
and Mies van der Rohe's
Barcelona chair (1929)
accompany an Eilersen
modular sofa, offering

a choice of seating, while
the small Eames table
adds flexibility to the
arrangement. The floor
lamp is Arne Jacobsen's
AJ Visor (1957).

Below — These teak-framed
chairs and sofa have a
mid-century modern appeal.

SITTING COMFORTABLY

To a large degree, what makes
a living area a relaxing place to be is
comfortable seating. However, one size
doesn't fit all, and your own definition
of comfort will differ from the next
person's. This is as much to do with
preference as it is body type. Some
people like to sink down into squashy
cushions; others would prefer to have
more support.

Sofas

Large items of furniture such as sofas
don't come cheap and their size means
that they will necessarily dominate
a room. Spend time researching the
market and don't commit to a purchase
before visiting a showroom or store to
try out the sofa in person. The angle of
the back, depth of the seat and height
of the armrests are key considerations.

Opt for the best quality you can
afford. Sofas that are well sprung and
soundly constructed may cost more
than mass-market alternatives, but
they will last much longer. Similarly,
look out for simple, clean silhouettes
and classic shapes that won't date. Solid
colours are a good bet for upholstery
– white and off-white, grey and blue are
recessive shades and visually minimize
bulk. Plain upholstery can always
be dressed up with a throw or quilt;
washable loose covers are another
practical way of ringing the changes.

Modular and sectional seating

Appealingly mid-century modern
in style, modular and sectional seating
can be assembled in a variety of
configurations to suit the size and shape
of your living area. Elements can be
added over time, which helps spread
the cost. Different permutations include
benches, sections with backrests and
side sections with back- and/or
armrests, like contemporary chaises
longues. Many types of modular seating
are flush with the ground; those on
raised legs are more space-enhancing
because the floor is not concealed.

Chairs

Their undoubted personalities explain
why many of us have our favourite
chairs. Mine is the Karuselli (see page
103), which is not only an iconic design
but also one of the most comfortable
chairs I have ever sat in.

Where the three-piece suite can be
a little deadening in effect (two facing
sofas are preferable), a grouping of
different chairs is hospitable. From the
upholstered armchair to the classic club
chair, from the rocker to the upright-
side chair, variations on the basic theme
add a sense of liveliness and character.
Casual seating for when you are
entertaining and there aren't enough
chairs to go around include stacking
stools, slatted folding chairs, floor
cushions and upholstered benches.

KARUSELLI

CHAIR

I have to declare a special interest in this example of iconic Finnish design by Yrjö Kukkapuro (b. 1933). It is simply my favourite place to sit because it is so comfortable. Shaped to echo the form of the human body, the Karuselli chair (1964–5) was supposedly inspired by an occasion when the designer was playing outside with his daughter making snow chairs. The original prototype consisted of chicken wire mounted on a steel frame and covered in canvas dipped in plaster. The process of development took a year. The design was an immediate international success when it appeared on the front cover of *Domus* in 1966.

Any chair where you sit for an extended period of time has to allow movement. The Karuselli both swivels and rocks. The seat shell and base are made of fibreglass-reinforced polyester; upholstery is white, black or tan leather. A chrome-plated steel spring and rubber dampers connect the seat to the base. Altogether it is a highly pleasing blend of the functional, the ergonomic and the organic.

Previous page — Rugs often make good starting places for living room colour schemes. The warm pinks, oranges and reds on the cushion covers echo the same shades in the flat-weave kilim.

Left — Soft furnishings contribute to a sense of comfort and relaxation. The filmy cotton drapery threaded along a pole softly diffuses the light. The white pleated paper pendants are by Le Klint.

Below — White walls and pale flooring make the most of the natural light spilling in through the glazed end wall of this living room, while a simple fabric blind (shade) screens glare.

LIGHTING

Natural light

A room flooded with natural light is a feel-good factor of the first order. Any space that is well lit, preferably from two aspects, will seem more spacious and more welcoming. South-facing rooms (north-facing in the southern hemisphere) benefit from a rich, warm light at the time of day when living areas are most likely to be used. Large mirrors hung opposite windows can spread natural light around.

Fabric window treatments – filmy curtains, crisp blinds (shades) and simple drapery – are more in keeping with the overall mood of relaxation than harder-edged Venetian blinds and are as efficient at preventing heat loss as they are at screening views after nightfall. Avoid fussy detailing and complicated headings and opt for plain, tailored effects.

Artificial light

Lighting should be planned carefully, as it can make or break a living room scheme. Bright, overhead light from a central source creates a bland, deadened atmosphere that throws shadows in the corners and shrinks the space. What you need instead is four to five separate sources of light, angled in different directions to create overlapping pools of light and shade. A key principle is to reflect light off the large expanses of walls and ceilings to accentuate a sense of volume.

○ Successful lighting schemes depend on a good infrastructure. Make sure you have enough power points positioned where you need them to avoid overloading sockets and trailing wires.

○ Although central light fixtures are popular in living areas because they provide a focus, it is important not to rely solely on them. Put pendants on a dimmer. Better still, choose chandeliers or similar branched fittings that have many individual points of light.

○ Table and floor lamps placed around the room draw the eye from place to place. A variety of heights, as much as positions, adds a sense of animation.

○ Recessed downlights work better in kitchens, bathrooms and hallways, where the layout is fixed, than they do in living areas, where you may want to change the furniture arrangement at some future date.

○ Wash the planes of walls and ceilings with light to enhance the sense of space. Use floor-standing uplighters or directional fittings such as spotlights or wall-washers. These will also enhance texture and architectural detail.

○ Highlight decorative displays with spotlights, picture lights or concealed striplighting.

○ Remember that the television is a light source itself. To avoid eye strain and glare, ensure that there isn't too great a contrast between the TV and the rest of the room.

GLO-BALL
LIGHT

The traditional floor-standing or 'standard' lamp, which typically featured a fabric or parchment shade, often fussily trimmed, was once a mainstay of living room lighting. This type of light fitting had been out of fashion for many years when it was reinterpreted and updated by a new generation of designers during the latter part of the twentieth century. The reason for its return to design favour is not difficult to see. While standard lamps do occupy a certain amount of floor area, they also allow you to vary the height of light sources and thus give an interior more of a lively quality.

The Glo-Ball (1999), by celebrated British designer Jasper Morrison (b. 1959), is a classic example of the floor lamp as sleek, minimal spatial marker. No less effective switched off than when it is illuminated, the Glo-Ball is one of a family of lamps that include pendants, tabletop and wall-mounted versions. The shade is a hand-blown, acid-etched glass diffuser, and the base and stem are made of white powdered stainless steel. The purity of the design is somewhat softened by its childlike appeal.

FOCAL POINTS

Most living areas are essentially unfitted spaces, which means that the furniture arrangement tends to define the layout. To give a layout cohesion – to pull the space together – you need to provide some sort of focal point.

In many homes, by default, this is the television screen. While there is no getting away from the fact that the TV is going to be a focal point when it is switched on and you are watching it, when it is off, its blank presence can give a room an air of passivity, like a cinema between screenings. These days, TV screens are so thin and flat that they are easy to conceal in a built-in cupboard or behind a panel so that they do not dominate a living area unnecessarily. An alternative is to put the TV on a mobile stand that can be brought into view when you want to watch a programme and pushed to one side the rest of the time.

Rugs

A focal point doesn't have to be at eye level. Rugs are an excellent way of tying things together and visually anchoring a grouping of sofa and chairs. Where the rest of the decoration and furnishing is plain and restrained, rugs can also inject a welcome accent of colour, pattern and texture, less insistently because they are underfoot.

Coffee tables

A low central table is the lynchpin of a conversation group. Getting the size right is important: too large and extensive and it will have the effect of pushing an arrangement apart instead of drawing it together; too small and it might as well not be there.

Avoid overelaborate designs. Glass-topped tables are self-effacing. Long, low benches in solid wood have a pleasing integrity. A grouping of small tables or stools is another versatile arrangement.

Fireplaces

In older houses, original fireplaces make natural focal points, even if we are no longer dependent on the warmth and light they provide. An open fire delivers all-round sensory pleasure, with the evocative smell and sound being as delightfully engaging as the way it looks and the cosy feeling it engenders.

The modern alternative is the solid-fuel stove. With its sculptural form, it makes a striking interjection into a contemporary space; bright colour is also an option. Unlike open fires, where a large proportion of the heat produced goes straight up the chimney, closed stoves are a very efficient way to heat a space.

Left — For graphic impact, it is hard to beat this arrangement of woodburning stove and caches for logs inset into the wall.

Below — Scatter cushions and a throw add comfort and visual interest to a plain sofa, while the quirky hand-carved stools make a charming accompaniment to a simple wooden coffee table.

Overleaf — Shelved alcoves at one end of the living room in our mews house combine storage for reference books with decorative displays, grouped together to provide visual delight without clutter.

Left — Propping a collection of prints on narrow shelving allows you to experiment with arrangement and ring the changes when you grow tired of the display.

Right — The mantelpiece, which is at eye level, is a natural location for an arrangement. Colours that repeat in the prints and objects on show provide a subtle unifying theme.

VISUAL DELIGHT

Creating visual delight – giving the eye something to dwell on – plays an important role in generating a mood of relaxation and a sense of welcome in living areas. Take the opportunity to play with scale and proportion – a large framed picture or mirror naturally commands attention, but so, too, does a sensitive grouping of objects – on this level, delight is the type of mental unwinding that is akin to staring into space or gazing out of the window at a beautiful view. Colour echoes, sculptural forms and the pattern inherent in a collection all serve to beguile the eye over and over again.

Aside from decorative objects, paintings and pictures, visual delight can also be supplied by soft furnishings, such as blankets and throws, scatter cushions and other accessories that are inexpensive to acquire and easy to change. Here is the opportunity to enjoy the accent of colour, to revel in textural variety or to play around with pattern without making a large-scale commitment. Changing such details from time to time – or perhaps even

seasonally – instantly refreshes a living area, especially when the rest of the decoration and furnishing is relatively low key and neutral.

Most transient of all, yet immensely appealing, are 'living' displays of fresh flowers and flourishing plants. I am not talking about florists' contrived arrangements, but generous bunches of whatever is in season, all the better if scent is involved.

Collections

You don't have to be a magpie, with an insatiable appetite for acquiring lots of things, to enjoy the simple pleasures of creating and displaying collections. Nor does what you collect have to have any great investment potential or inherent worth. What counts is your delight in what you collect and your willingness to share this with others.

HERE ARE A FEW RULES FOR DISPLAY

Bring it all together

○

Don't dot pictures and objects here, there and everywhere.
Decide on a location and group them together so that the
collection reads as a whole. This looks far less busy and
intrusive and maximizes impact.

Group like with like

○

Displays are more powerful when there is an underlying
theme. This might be type of object, colour, pattern or texture,
form or material.

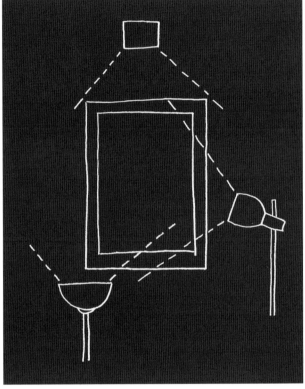

Variety is the spice of life

○

Informal collections – objects grouped on a shelf or tabletop, pictures propped on a mantelpiece – are easy to change when you grow tired of them.

Consider lighting

○

Enhance a collection with directional spotlights, uplighting, side-lighting or backlighting.

STORAGE

In any area of the home, clutter is stressful. This is especially true of living areas, where we ought to be able to unwind without nagging reminders of chores left undone, or having to pick our way through muddle and mess to locate the remote control. A little untidiness is only to be expected – and welcomed as evidence of human life – but serious disorder needs tackling head on.

In multipurpose living areas – those that double up as home offices or eating areas – the need for good organization is even more acute. Think about whether any of the belongings you normally keep in the living area could be decanted somewhere else – your library of books to an adjacent hallway, for example. For the remainder, the best solution is often to exploit wall space for shelving and concealed built-in storage. You can store a great many belongings in one room and maintain a sense of comfort and ease provided the floor is kept clear.

Storage furniture

Contemporary storage furniture is a far cry from the clunky, heavy, space-devouring breakfronts and sideboards of days gone by. Low cabinets in glossy lacquered metal or sleek veneered wood, freestanding modular space dividers and open shelving can all house a variety of possessions while usefully serving to demarcate different areas of activity.

Containers

While baskets, lidded boxes, trunks and such like hide clutter from view, they shouldn't be used as catch-alls for belongings that lack a settled home or are waiting for the rainy day when you will get down to sorting through them. Containers such as these are most effective as a means of storing similar items together, either on open shelving or within cupboards.

Shelving and built-in storage

Without doubt, shelving is one of the most practical options for organizing collections of books, magazines, CDs, DVDs and the other accessories of home entertainment. With a little forethought, it can be stylish, too.

○ Floating shelving – painted shelves cantilevered from the wall on concealed fixings – is robust and reads as part of the structure of the room.

○ A wholehearted approach, where entire walls are devoted to shelving, is much more appealing than a few shelves put here and there. Work with the room's basic layout and make use of alcoves and other recessed features.

○ Use shelves for horizontal emphasis within a space. Low shelving along the length of a wall has a contemporary feel, while the top shelf can double up as a place for casual seating or display.

○ Keep unsightly objects behind closed doors and incorporate areas of closed storage for items that do not contribute much to the character of the space. Flush floor-to-ceiling panels can be used to screen home offices, files and supplies discreetly and minimally.

Entertainment

While entertainment systems have become even more minimal and unobtrusive, that does not solve the problem of what to do with films and music you used to watch or listen to in formats that are now redundant. Nor has the potential for photographs, films, music and books to be stored digitally severed some people's affection for the physical object, whether this is a cherished vinyl record or a hardback book. What is clear, however, is that if you hang onto several versions of the same piece of entertainment, your living area is going to resemble a multimedia store instead of a place to relax.

○ Be discriminating. Get rid of anything you are unlikely to watch or listen to again. Those films and albums you want to keep should be in the latest, most compact version. This frees you to get rid of old video recorders, for example – or at least to store them remotely.

○ Back up your digital collections. Store space-devouring digital files of photographs, films and music on a separate hard drive.

○ Control cabling so that power points aren't overloaded and wires aren't trailing everywhere.

Children's play

Given the opportunity, children will play almost anywhere in the home – not merely in their own rooms, but also in the kitchen, on the stairs, in your bedroom, under the dining table and, of course, in the living room. Part of the joy of family life is togetherness – and one of its necessities is having space you can call your own.

This is not to suggest that living areas should be child-free zones until the kids have grown up a little – simply that you make things easier for yourself in the early days of parenthood by providing dedicated places to store toys at the end of the day. This should be in close proximity to where they are most commonly played with. You don't want to be scooping up an armful of Lego from the living room floor to return it to your child's bedroom every evening. Far better to provide a container on a shelf or in a cupboard in the living room where it can be tidied away quickly.

Similarly, when sticky fingers (and muddy paw prints) are the norm, make sure that living room furnishings are detachable and washable and that rugs and carpets have been treated for stain-resistance.

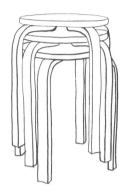

MODEL № 60

STOOL

Beguilingly simple, sturdy and versatile, the three-legged stool designed by the great Finnish architect Alvar Aalto (1898–1976) was first put into production in 1933. Aalto designed furniture for many of his buildings and the stool was originally conceived for the Viipuri Library (now the Vyborg Library in Russia), which was completed in 1935.

The key element of the stool is the bent L-shaped leg, which arose out of Aalto's experiments with Otto Korhonen, the technical director of a furniture factory. The process is basically the same today. Solid birch is left to season, then sawn in the direction of the grain so that it forms a fan-shape. Thin pieces of birch veneer are then slotted into the grooves and the wood is bent through 90 degrees using heat and steam. The result is a leg that can be attached directly to the underside of the seat without any need of a supporting framework, making the entire piece easy to construct.

Today the stool is available in natural or lacquered birch and with different coloured tops. It is still produced by Artek, co-founded by Aalto with the express purpose to bring 'a human perspective to modernism'. Readily stackable, it performs equally well as a side table as occasional seating.

PLAIN

SIMPLE

USEFUL
---
working

Left — Working areas may
have to be practical and
productive places, but style
shouldn't take a back seat.
The vivid orange of my desk
gives me pleasure, as does the

quirky storage unit fashioned
from wooden crates held
together with plastic clips.

working

Working at home comes in many guises – from the overtime you put in to complete a project out of office hours to the burgeoning career you pursue from a self-contained study or annexe. Then there are all the chores that go along with running a household, from cleaning and doing the laundry to tackling everyday administration. Paid or unpaid, routine or occasional, what all of these tasks require are good systems of organization and careful planning to accommodate them within a domestic setting.

Style, however, is far from a side issue. If your home office has been decorated, equipped and furnished in such a way that spending time there is a pleasure, you are more likely to be productive. If utility areas are not scruffy afterthoughts, daily chores will seem less of an imposition. Even the smallest working areas, such as broom cupboards and linen closets, can have a certain down-to-earth charm if they are fitted out with care and attention. It is the same pleasing sense of usefulness that is conveyed by an old-fashioned hardware store.

Right — Computer-based work does not need to take up much space. A little psychological separation is necessary, however. Here a compact work area has been set up in front of a window.

Far right — Bedrooms are probably not the best places for long periods of concentrated work. But George Nelson's Swag Leg desk (1958), a writing table with bright cubbyholes, makes a stylish place to catch up on emails and correspondence. The DSR chair (1950) is by Eames.

SHARED WORKING AREAS

In theory, a laptop and a wireless connection mean that it is possible to work anywhere in the home – in bed, at the kitchen table or sitting on the sofa. But, just as the arrival of the computer did not lead to paperless offices, portable technology has not lessened the need for a settled workspace. You can catch up on your emails anywhere, but for extensive periods of concentrated work, a dedicated workspace is essential.

If spatial limitations are such that the only way of accommodating a home office is to commandeer part of a living area or bedroom, you need to ensure that the space functions equally well in both capacities, both practically and aesthetically. In many cases, that calls for some sort of built-in arrangement.

Compact study areas can be slotted into a working wall of storage so that they can be screened from view behind flush panels when they are not in use. Pull-out or fold-down desktops mean that you do not need to sacrifice too much floor area to create such a fitted feature – a shelf's width will do.

ANGLEPOISE
LIGHT

The classic Anglepoise (1932) was the first-ever freestanding adjustable task light, and arguably remains the best. The inspiration of British automotive engineer George Cawardine (1887–1947), it makes use of springs to anchor the jointed metal arms to the base, the articulation a clear reference to the anatomy of human limbs. While it was Cawardine's idea that springs would provide the required degree of flexibility, along with the counterweighted tension that would keep the light in its adjusted position, it was a spring manufacturer, Herbert Terry & Sons, who spotted the potential of the patented design to market their products. The result was a successful move into production, where the design, in various versions, has remained ever since. Like 'hoover', the trade name 'anglepoise' has become a generic term.

While the original design had a shade and arm made of lacquered metal and a Bakelite base, today the light is all metal. It comes in a choice of colours and with either a solid base or a screw clamp for fixing it to the side of a drawing board.

Left — Surprisingly effective workplaces can be set up in out-of-the-way areas of the home, such as halls and general circulation spaces. This concealed cupboard with integral lighting provides room for a worktop and shelving for files and other necessities.

Below — Free space under the stairs has been simply furnished with a plain table, task light and pair of chairs.

BORROWED SPACE

In older homes, the circulation areas of hallways and landings can be very generous – wastefully so to modern eyes. Another 'between' space that is often ripe for exploitation is the area under the stairs. Somewhat set apart, these areas provide a degree of psychological separation from the rest of the household and can usefully serve as compact working areas with the addition of recessed lighting, built-in shelving and worktops. If possible, choose a location that benefits from a good quality of natural light. However, such borrowed spaces, unless they are very extensive, are probably best for occasional use. You won't be able to spread out or make much of a creative mess.

In lofts or live/work spaces with high ceilings, an alternative is to exploit spatial volume and subdivide the area vertically. Mezzanines don't have to be very extensive to be effective, but they do require solid and robust means of access if they are in regular use. Depending on available head-height, you can either set up your office on the top or treat the new level as a sleeping platform and work underneath.

Below — Ample storage, good natural light and plenty of peace and quiet add up to ideal conditions for creative work. If you are running your own business from home, a dedicated study or workspace is essential to prevent household distractions from adversely affecting your productivity.

Right — If your work is chiefly desk-bound, you won't necessarily need a great deal of floor area. This compact study features a built-in worktop and shelves.

Overleaf — More of a home studio than study, this large, bright, airy workspace means business. With room for relaxing, extensive built-in storage and lots of natural light flooding in through the arched double windows, such a setting makes work a pleasure.

STUDIES

A study of one's own is high on the list of most people's priorities. Such private retreats, where you can close the door on the rest of the household, are deeply appealing. More than that, they are essential if you are earning your living at home, as many people are these days, or if your occupation necessarily requires more space than that taken up by a laptop and printer.

An element of horse-trading is bound to go on regarding which notional 'spare' room can be pressed into service as a home office or study. But the answer is not always to choose the smallest of available options. It is also important to spend the time and effort to furnish the space sympathetically and with a degree of character. A home workspace does not have to resemble the one-size-fits-all corporate environment.

In recent years the humble garden shed has been reincarnated as the ultimate location for working from home. With a short commute down the garden providing the necessary mental separation, these outbuildings have become increasingly attractive and sophisticated. Many off-the-shelf designs come ready-insulated and equipped with electrical connections.

Below — Twin wall-mounted Bestlites provide dedicated task lighting for a worktop. While you need angled task lighting to highlight the page or computer keyboard in front of you, uplighting provides good general background illumination.

Right — Make room for inspiration. A collection of prints and decorative objects provides food for thought in a simple working area that forms part of an open-plan living space. The floor-standing lamp can be positioned as need dictates.

LIGHTING

As with all lighting schemes, when it comes to lighting the hardworking areas of your home, planning is key. Targeted task lighting is essential to ensure that the space is both functional and comfortable to be in.

○ For work that is essentially desk- or computer-based, you will need much higher levels of light than for general relaxing – up to five times more. One or two task lights that can be angled to direct light at the page or keyboard are essential. Make sure the bulb is well shaded to avoid the risk of glare.

○ You can't rely on task lighting alone because the contrast between your desktop (virtual or otherwise) and your surroundings will be too great, resulting in eye strain. Uplights that bounce light off the ceiling are effective sources of background light, as they do not cause reflections or shadows on the computer screen.

○ Wherever possible, site a working area where it will benefit from good natural light – toplighting from rooflights and skylights promotes an expansive quality that is ideal for creative thought. Natural light, preferably north light, is essential for any work that involves making accurate colour judgements.

○ Utility areas, such as laundry rooms, are about the only places where a single overhead light source is acceptable. Workshops are a different matter. If your workroom incorporates a toolbench, striplighting mounted on a shelf directly above and concealed behind a baffle will give you task light where you need it.

TRESTLE

TABLE

The trestle table is a furniture type that dates back at least as far as the Middle Ages and even precedes the refectory table with its fixed frame. Comprising nothing more elaborate than a board or planks propped on top of A-framed wooden supports, it could be easily moved, disassembled and stored away. There are many contemporary variations on the basic trestle theme, from rough-and-ready versions, such as those used by decorators and paper-hangers, to more refined and elegant examples that can usefully double up as dining tables, whenever the two activities of eating and working take place in the same area. Those with glass tops are particularly space-enhancing.

My own trestle table, which I use for work meetings at my house in the country, is the Leonardo by the renowned Italian designer Achille Castiglioni (1918–2002). It dates from 1940 and is still produced today by Zanotta. The adjustable trestles are made from solid beech finished with a natural varnish; the top is white laminate with matching beech lippings.

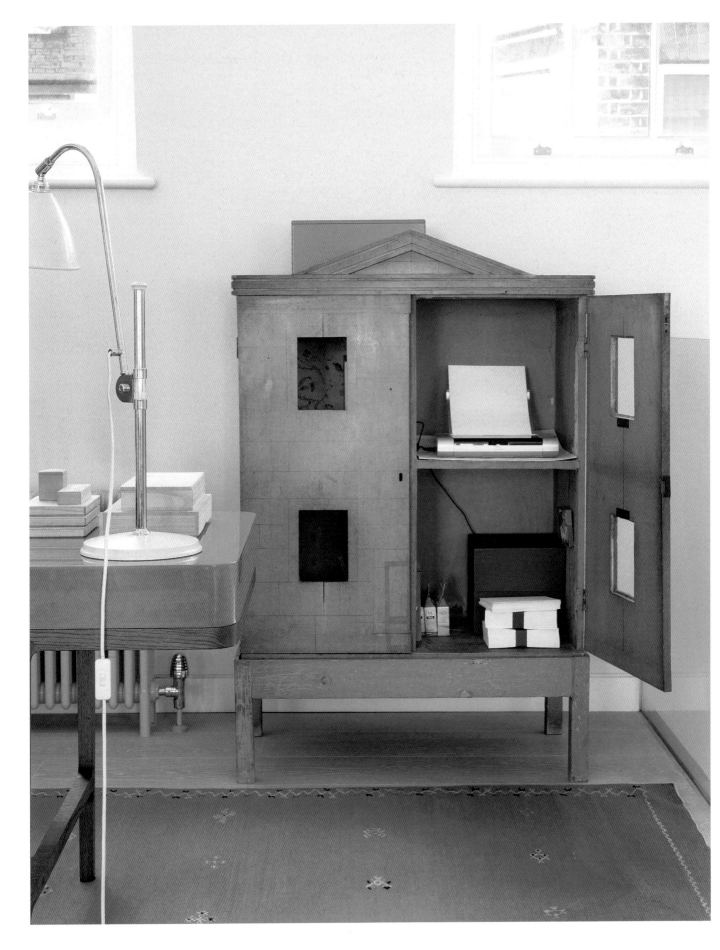

Left — A far cry from the regulation steel office cupboard, this antique doll's house serves as a place to keep bulk supplies of paper and a printer.

Below — The EA117 office chair (1958) by Charles and Ray Eames is an ergonomic design that looks as good as it feels. Soft leather upholstery is mounted on an aluminium frame. The chair can be tilted, is height-adjustable and moves freely on castors.

EQUIPMENT

Work chairs

If your work entails sitting for long periods, you need to equip yourself with a desk chair that has been designed along ergonomic principles. It is not simply a question of selecting an example that provides adequate support and which can be adjusted in height to accommodate different body types. Trouble can flair up when you sit in a chair that traps you in the same position hour after hour. For this reason, ergonomic chairs permit natural shifts of posture, such as tilting and leaning. You may need to search a little harder for designs whose appearance matches performance. The Eames office chair is one that springs to mind.

Work tables and desks

For the home office that forms part of a multipurpose space or which must double up as an eating area for part of the time, generic pieces, such as simple trestle or refectory tables, which don't proclaim themselves as office furniture, are the best option. Glass-topped tables are unobtrusive.

There is more scope if your working area is self-contained. You can take inspiration from classic mid-century modern designs, such as George Nelson's writing table, with its vividly coloured pigeonholes, and look out for a desk with contemporary flair or treat yourself to a vintage find.

Below — Routine household
chores can almost become
pleasurable if you take the
time and effort to equip your
utility areas with a degree of
care and thought. Here the

appliances are stacked on top
of one another next to a sink
specifically for hand-washing,
with all the relevant cleaning
products close at hand on
shelves above.

Below right — Racking or
suspending tools from hooks
is a simple and effective way
of organizing them – far
better than chucking them in
a broom cupboard willy-nilly.

UTILITY ROOMS

Hardworking areas behind the scenes,
utility rooms are often overlooked and
under-planned. This is not to say that
you should kit them out with the same
care and attention that you would
bestow on a living room, for example,
but that even functional space benefits
from attention to detail. Neat and
cheerful working areas make chores
seem less like drudgery.

Lately there has been a revival of
interest in proper household tools, such
as traditional brooms and brushes with
natural bristles and wooden handles,
or enamelled and metal hardware, such
as buckets and washing basins. These
items are not only fit for purpose, but
they also have a simple charm all of
their own. But, like the serious cook
who becomes a little too enamoured of
gadgetry to the detriment of available
storage space, it is possible to go

overboard in this department, too.
You don't need a selection of brushes
that each performs a specific task, for
instance, when a decent soft brush and
hard brush will tackle most jobs.

Shared
In households that are short of space,
utility areas often form part of kitchens
or bathrooms, rooms that are already
serviced and plumbed. Where to site
appliances needs careful planning.

Below — Wall-hung wooden storage lockers make good stowing places for outdoor kit, sports equipment and garden tools.

Below right — Portable baskets for linen and cleaning products organize like with like and can be readily moved from place to place.

In a kitchen, for example, you don't want to interrupt the natural workflow involved in cooking and preparing food; in a bathroom, you need to ensure that there is sufficient space for other fixed points in the layout. Adequate ventilation is essential in both cases. Look out for appliances that are relatively quiet in operation.

Separate

The separate utility room is the present-day incarnation of the old scullery, where the heavy-duty washing and scrubbing used to take place. The temptation in many cases is to install the appliances and let the rest of the space look after itself. This is to miss the opportunity to provide the extra degree of finesse that makes routine household tasks almost enjoyable. Shelving or built-in cupboards can be used to house cleaning products, washing powders or bulk supplies. Racks and peg rails help to organize cleaning tools, brooms and brushes.

The same principle should extend to the smallest working area of all – the broom cupboard. If you throw everything in there haphazardly, you instantly add muddle to housework. Instead, make use of the back of the door to organize small items on shallow shelves or on racks.

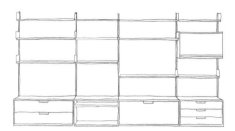

606 UNIVERSAL
SHELVING SYSTEM

Flexible, adaptable, robust and self-effacing, the 606 Universal Shelving System (1960) is everything you want storage to be. Rightly considered to be a modern classic and in continuous production for more than half a century, the system was designed by the legendary Dieter Rams (b. 1932), who headed Braun's creative team from 1961 to 1995 and who still works in an advisory capacity for Vitsoe, the company that supplies and makes the 606.

The ultimate in modular design, the system has at its core the aluminium 'E-track' that fixes directly to the wall. Shelves, cabinets and tables then simply hang from the track on notched aluminium pins. For uneven walls, the E-tracks can be attached to posts; alternatively, if there is no convenient wall space, the posts can be compressed between floor and ceiling and the tracks attached to their sides. Hidden tracking can make cabinets and drawers appear to float.

The system is a true kit of parts. Elements are interchangeable and can be reconfigured according to what you need to store and the space you have available. Because the specification has remained the same, you can also add to the system as need dictates in future years.

STORAGE
- - - - - - - - - - - -

The plain, simple and useful approach to living is not about self-denial or adopting an extreme form of minimalism. But it does mean exercising your critical judgement so that your home is not overwhelmed with redundant clutter. If you are cooking, for example, and you have to hunt around for the right ingredient, that wastes time. But when you are earning your living from home, muddle can cost you more than frustration.

There are three main levels of storage: items you need to keep directly at hand; those that you need to access on an occasional basis; and things that can be consigned to deep storage and put away in a remote location, such as an attic or basement. Everything else is surplus to requirements.

At hand

Whatever you keep on your desktop or worktable or on shelving in its immediate vicinity should be in daily use. This includes paperwork and reference material involving current projects, recent bills and household administration, and anything else that falls into the category of 'pending'.

Ideally, your desktop should be as clear as possible. If this is not possible, a shallow wooden in-tray is a simple and stylish way of keeping essential documents to hand.

Similarly, cleaning products that are used on a daily basis should be kept close to where you need them and separate from others, such as silver polish, stain removers and floor seals, that you only need once in a while to tackle some specific job.

Nearby

For items that you need occasionally but regularly, create working walls of storage with cupboards, open shelving or modular units, either in the working area itself or adjacent to it. Built-in storage is more discreet. Otherwise paint shelves the same colour as the walls or choose contemporary freestanding shelving in wood or steel. An array of coordinated box files or containers organizes paperwork and keeps the contents dust-free. Candidates for this level of storage include:

○ Files relating to your recent work history, going back no further than a couple of years.
○ Invoices, accounts and tax returns relating to a similar period.
○ Instruction manuals, insurance documents and other types of household admin.
○ Printer paper and other supplies.
○ Reference material that you need to consult regularly.

Remote

Attics, basements and other out-of-the-way spaces are ideal places for stowing belongings or records that you don't want to dispose of but do not need to use or refer to very often. Here, the important consideration is making sure that the location provides adequate keeping conditions: dry and as dust-free as possible. Even so, robust lidded containers, ideally made of plastic, are preferable to open shelves or cardboard boxes.

Make a list or inventory of whatever you put into deep storage – out of sight is all too often out of mind. Set aside time to regularly sift through what you have stored and discard anything that has since become redundant. Tax returns, for example, only need to be kept for a certain number of years and then they can be shredded.

Display

One of the advantages of working from home is that it offers you the chance to move away from a soulless office environment. Make some room near your desk for images that inspire you – postcards or photographs tacked on a pinboard – perhaps a vase of fresh flowers and a memento or two.

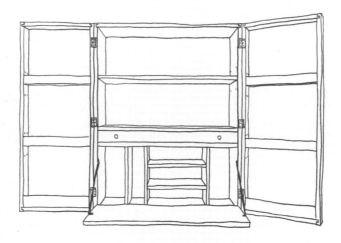

PROJECT #2

STATIONERY CUPBOARD

The second of the projects I have specifically designed for this book is a stationery cupboard. Laptops, iPads and other electronic devices may be increasingly how most of us work and communicate these days, but I am certain I am not alone in relishing the way creative ideas seem to flow when you are putting pen or pencil to paper. A clear desktop is also a prerequisite of uninterrupted thought, so this cabinet has been designed to house all the bits and bobs that otherwise might clutter up your worktable.

The inspiration behind the fitting-out of the cupboard has been taken from the interior arrangements of classic pieces of storage furniture, such as partner's desks and secretaires, with their appealing array of little drawers and neat pigeonholes. Shallow wooden shelves on the two hinged doors provide a means of holding small items and drawing pads so that they can be seen at a glance and readily retrieved. The body of the cupboard features vertical and horizontal subdivisions for organizing notepaper, envelopes and writing and drawing implements, along with a pull-out drawer and a fold-down flap for note-taking. Full step-by-step instructions on how to make the cupboard can be viewed online at www.octopusbooks.co.uk/psu.

PLAIN

SIMPLE

USEFUL

----

sleeping

sleeping

First and foremost, the bedroom should be a restorative haven where you can unwind. Unlike living areas and kitchens, which are on public view, the bedroom is a private space and should be treated as such. The difficulty is that in homes where there is great pressure on space, other functions tend to encroach upon its central role and compromise it. If you need to accommodate your entire wardrobe, set up a workstation, or house part of your library in your bedroom, you will need careful planning (and decent storage) to preserve the essential mood of peace and quiet.

Nothing should stand between you and a good night's sleep – no distracting clutter, no overflowing wardrobes, no dust-catching knick-knacks. Instead you should concentrate your attention on getting the basics right: the quality of light and air, the bed linen that goes next to your skin, and the bed itself.

Children's rooms are a slightly different proposition. In the early years, they double up as play spaces; later on, they generally have to accommodate study areas, so building in flexibility is essential.

BEDS

The bed is undoubtedly a dominant item of furniture. It not only occupies a considerable amount of floor area, but it also has to be centrally placed to allow access from both sides and make changing the sheets easier. Given this prominence, there is really no need to choose a bed that makes an elaborate style statement. It is far better to keep it simple and unfussy.

Simplest of all are divan beds that sit directly on the floor. Some versions incorporate deep drawers in the base, which can be useful places for storing spare bed linen, blankets or bulky sweaters, particularly when space is tight. An addition of a headboard, padded or otherwise, adds to the comfort of reading in bed.

There is also a wide choice of plain bed frames, ranging from variations on the classic brass bedstead in painted metal to elegant contemporary designs in wood. Beds with legs, however short, are inherently more space-enhancing because the floor area is not interrupted. Headboards that extend on either side to form integral night tables also have a pleasing neatness.

Mattresses

The most important element of the bed is the mattress. This is what provides the support and determines comfort. While you can economize on bed frames or bedsteads (although not to the point of flimsiness), you should buy the best-quality mattress you can afford, which generally means a pocketed sprung mattress of some kind. Be prepared to change it every ten years or so. Most mattresses should be turned regularly to distribute wear evenly.

As with major pieces of upholstered furniture, such as sofas, you should take the time to visit a showroom and try out different mattresses in person, preferably with your partner. This is not a purchase that can be made online.

A mattress that is too hard will put pressure on your joints and throw your hips and shoulders out of alignment so that your spine is not straight; one that is too soft will make it more difficult for you to make the minor movements that naturally occur during sleep. Either way, back problems can result. Perceived softness and hardness is a function of your body weight; if you and your partner have very different frames, you may need a mattress that provides a different degree of support on each side.

Left — Simple lightweight
drapery at the windows
screens views and protects
privacy during the daytime,
with heavier outer curtains

blocking out any unwelcome
light and providing greater
warmth and better sound
insulation at night.

Below — Pale-toned décor
keeps the overall effect of this
bedroom light and spacious.
Conversely, cramped
surroundings, bright colours,

fussy patterns and detailing
can be overstimulating,
making it difficult to sleep.

LIGHTING

Natural light

It is important to pay attention to the quality of light in bedrooms, even though we will be unconscious for most of the time we are in them. Natural light has a profound effect on our circadian rhythms: it sets our body clocks. Unless you are one of those people who need total darkness to drop off to sleep, translucent window treatments – lightweight drapery or cotton blinds (shades) – will screen views and protect privacy while allowing the stimulus of morning light to shine through. Adjustable louvred blinds (shades) are also very effective and generate moody bands of light and shade.

A good quality of natural light also goes hand in hand with a sense of spaciousness. Light colours, and surfaces and finishes that are light in tone – such as pale wood flooring, natural-fibre coverings or neutral carpeting and smooth white or off-white walls – make the most of whatever light the bedroom receives, and spread it around. Unlike other areas of the home, where pale or all-white décor can be impractical, the bedroom is not an area of heavy traffic or round-the-clock use.

Artificial light

Bedroom lighting should never be an afterthought. Spend some time planning the arrangement and organizing infrastructure at the outset, to ensure that you build in an element of flexibility. You will need a decent level of overall background illumination as well as brighter task lighting for reading in bed.

○ Avoid relying solely on a bright central overhead fixture. This deadens the atmosphere and causes glare when you are lying down. Multiple light sources generate a much more welcoming and relaxing mood.

○ If your bedroom is on the small side, judiciously placed uplights that direct light at the ceiling can enhance a sense of spaciousness and provide soft, ambient illumination.

○ Lighting that is concealed behind the headboard, under the bed, or under built-in cupboards creates a diffusing glow that makes such dominant features appear to float in space.

○ Put lights on dimmers so that you can adjust levels according to the time of day. If possible, ensure that lights can be controlled by switches both at the door and beside the bed.

○ A pair of shaded table lights or wall-mounted lights on each side of the bed provide illumination for reading. Ideally, you should be able to angle these so that they direct light straight at the page.

○ Built-in wardrobes and closets benefit from interior information lights that let you review what you own and locate items easily.

○ When children are very young, avoid table or floor lamps with wires that can be tugged.

BED LINEN

Fibres

There is nothing so appealing as the feeling of clean, crisp bed linen next to the skin. Natural fibres, such as cotton and linen, are highly absorbent; by wicking moisture away from the skin they help to control the body's temperature. Smoothest of all is bed linen made of Egyptian long-staple cotton, particularly that with a high thread count. Blends, where synthetic fibres such as polyester are added to the mix for a variety of practical reasons – easy maintenance and so on – may be cheaper but are much less comfortable.

Colour and pattern

For purists, white sheets, pillowcases and duvet covers are the ultimate in bedroom luxury. Soft blues, greys and off-whites, which are distancing, recessive shades, are better choices than vivid colour if you don't want pure white. An alternative is to opt for bed linen that incorporates a textured effect in the weave – a jacquard or seersucker, for example – or to add colour and pattern accents with occasional blankets, quilts and throws.

Pillows

Once pillows lose their shape and thus their capacity to support the head and neck, they should be replaced.

○ Down-filled pillows are the softest and most expensive.
○ Feather-and-down pillows are the most resilient.
○ Synthetic foam or fibre pillows are advisable if you suffer from allergies.

THE

DUVET

Strange as it may seem today, there was a time when bed-making was a significant chore, demanding an element of expertise in the fashioning of neat hospital corners. That was before the duvet.

The duvet – the term comes from the French word for 'down' – was alien to Britain when I first started selling them in Habitat in the early 1960s. I had first come across them during a trip to Sweden in the 1950s and had been amazed at how simple and labour-saving they were. Our initial campaign focused on the advantages of the 'ten-second bed' and, although initially we sold more single duvets than doubles, the 'continental quilt' gradually took off. Now it is rare to find anyone who still sleeps under sheets and blankets.

Duvets are thought to have originated in rural Europe, although no one knows precisely when. Early examples were generally stuffed with down from the eider duck. Nowadays, there are many different fillings, from duck- and goose-feather blends to synthetics. Best of all, however, is the all-goose-feather duvet, which is light and supremely warm.

I am glad to say that we have recently designed a duvet cover with a seersucker finish that doesn't need ironing, reducing time spent bed-making still further.

Left — A dedicated dressing area can be set up very compactly. This combination of hanging space, open shelves and wide drawers occupies a purpose-built freestanding

unit that doubles up as an effective spatial divider.

Below — Good use has been made of all the available space in this wholehearted approach to built-in storage. Cubbyholes and shelves for sweaters, shirts and shoes

have been slotted into what otherwise would be an awkward space.

CLOTHES STORAGE

While 'plain' and 'simple' may not necessarily apply to every item in your wardrobe, 'useful' almost certainly should. Don't waste space by storing clothes that you never wear – as much as 80 per cent of the average person's wardrobe in some estimates.

Set aside the time to go through your clothing on a regular basis – when the season changes is a natural time for review – and discard what you don't need. Not only will you gain more space, but also the clothes you have left will be kept in better conditions. Overstuffed drawers and hanging rails are breeding grounds for moths.

Another way of reducing the pressure on space – and making the bedroom a more relaxing place to be – is to rotate clothing in and out of remote storage according to the season. Pack away the clothes you don't need immediately in mothproof garment bags.

The next decision to make is whether to go the built-in or freestanding route, or a combination of the two. While much will depend on the amount of space at your disposal, built-in storage is generally more space-efficient and easier on the eye than a collection of different pieces of freestanding furniture; it can also be tailored to your needs. Whatever you do, don't keep clothes on open rails or shelves, where they will get dusty, become faded or be at greater risk from moth damage.

Built-in clothes-storage systems look best when they are approached in a wholehearted architectural fashion. This means fitting out an entire wall instead of a portion of one, and extending up to the ceiling instead of stopping at an indeterminate point beneath it. Avoid superfluous detailing and mouldings on door fronts – flush panels create a seamless backdrop and read as an uninterrupted plane. Bear in mind, too, that practicality means ease of operation: doors that press open and drawers, baskets or panels that slide effortlessly on runners.

○ Allow a depth of 600mm (23½in) for hanging storage. Double-hanging jackets, skirts and shirts makes maximum use of space.

○ Drawers require a clearance of 1m (3ft 3in) in front. Never fill a drawer more than two-thirds full.

○ Customize the interior of built-in storage with drawer dividers to organize small items, and with racks or rails for shoes, belts, ties and scarves.

○ The area under the bed can be used as additional storage space. Lidded plastic containers on wheels are ideal for shoes or bulky sweaters.

Below — Built-in or concealed storage keeps clothes in better condition than open rails and shelves where they are at greater risk of becoming dusty, faded and moth-eaten.

Below right — An array of cubbyholes houses an impressive collection of shirts. A full-length mirror is essential in dressing areas, as is good lighting.

Right — If you have sufficient space, it makes good sense to house your wardrobe outside the bedroom. This dressing area has been custom-built. Many companies offer designs for fitted storage that can be adapted to suit your specific requirements.

THE DRESSING ROOM

Housing your entire wardrobe in a separate dressing room may seem the height of spatial extravagance, but it can greatly improve the atmosphere and workability of the bedroom itself. You may not even need to sacrifice a separate room; an adjacent hallway or vestibule, if it is wide enough, will serve the same purpose just as well. Make sure that whichever location

you choose, it is near the bedroom or bathroom and offers a degree of privacy.

The most stylish solutions are often those that are custom-built. As with other forms of built-in storage, quality of materials and neatness of finish are all-important. If your budget stretches, opt for veneered or solid wood doors. Alternatives include semitranslucent acrylic panels and sliding screens.

You can either line facing walls with cupboards or extend built-in storage the entire length of a wall.

Dressing rooms can also be furnished with a system supplied by a storage specialist. These offer flexible designs with interiors that feature hanging space, shoe drawers and cubbyholes in different configurations. Interior lighting and a full-length mirror are essentials.

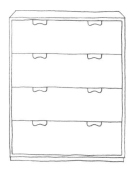

SNOW

CHEST OF DRAWERS

Part of a range of storage furniture that includes glass-fronted cabinets and wardrobes (closets), the Snow chest of drawers (1994) was designed by Thomas Sandell (b. 1959) and Jonas Bohlin (b. 1953). Sandell, a Finnish-born architect with a Finnish-Swedish background, is part of a new generation of Scandinavian designers who have turned their attention to producing beautiful things for everyday use. This range was designed around the same time that Sandell was collaborating closely with retail giant IKEA on their innovative PS products.

Solid, simple and soundly constructed, the Snow chest of drawers is manufactured by the Swedish company Asplund. Materials are lacquered MDF and solid birch; colours include soft neutral greys and light browns, along with white. The shaped drawer pulls add a certain softness to the design, while the drawers themselves are self-closing, an elegant ease of operation that lends pleasure to use. In keeping with the finest examples of mid-century Scandinavian modern, this piece combines functionality and sound craftsmanship with aesthetic restraint and a human touch.

Left— All children love to see their favourite things around them – less is not more. The small Componibili storage unit (1969) by Anna Castelli Ferrieri (see page 185) doubles up as a night table.

CHILDREN'S ROOMS

From the precious new arrival to the boisterous toddler, from the curious schoolchild to the moody teenager, children pass through successive stages at what seems like the blink of an eye. Keeping pace with such a rate of change demands flexibility and a certain degree of planning ahead.

While you can't expect a child's room to remain the same from babyhood to the day when your teenager flies the nest, you can make things easier on yourself and your wallet by adopting the plain, simple and useful approach. This entails restricting any element that is age-specific or themed – whether it is ducks and bunnies, a favourite cartoon character or a football team – to items that can be quickly and economically changed: soft furnishings rather than wallpaper, for example. By the same token, opt for simple, generic furniture that will last the course, instead of miniaturized nursery versions that will be outgrown quickly, and choose surfaces and finishes with an eye to easy maintenance and staying power, which means wipe-clean paint finishes, stain-resistant flooring, and materials that, generally, can take a bit of punishment and look all the better for it. It is not a question of imposing an adult sense of style on impressionable young minds, but of giving children the scope to express themselves within reasonable boundaries.

Room allocation

Babies don't need big rooms and most teenagers will accept a smaller room if that is what it takes to win them privacy. When children are young, however, and play is largely floor-based, it makes sense to give them a large bedroom and preferably one with a good quality of natural light.

Focus on safety

Avoid trailing wires, use socket covers over power points, anchor heavy furniture or freestanding bookcases securely to the wall and make sure upper-storey windows have locks. Platform or bunk beds should have robust ladders and should be used only by children over five or six.

Allow room for display

At every stage of development, children love to see their possessions and their creations on display, whether it is the familiar night-time line-up of soft toys, a treasured piece of their own artwork or posters featuring the current flavour of the month.

Lighting

Shade central pendants with paper lanterns or glass globes to avoid glare. Dimmer controls are useful in order to lower the light level for night-time feeds; night-lights provide reassurance for young children. Study areas will need adjustable wall lights or task lights.

Below — Children love
hidey-holes – window seats,
secret dens and treehouses.
This recessed box bed has
much of the same appeal,
with its tongue-and-groove

panelling concealing storage
caches and a large drawer
at the base.

Right — Twin beds, arranged
end to end along the length
of a bedroom wall, feature
drawers underneath for
storing bedding and clothes.
A sturdy wall-mounted

narrow shelving unit
organizes favourite toys,
books and games.

CHILDREN'S STORAGE

As children grow and develop, their
interests and abilities change – shifts
that are marked by the acquisition of
entirely new categories of possessions,
sometimes before they are ready to let
go of the old ones. Where once Lego
featured on every Christmas list, now
it is sports gear or the latest electronic
device or passing fashion. Keeping
ahead of the game means putting
flexible storage systems into place and
instigating regular and diplomatic
clear-outs of toys, games and books
that are past their sell-by date.

Early years

The stage when a young child's
possessions can be housed in a single
portable container is fairly short-lived.
Try to resist an ad-hoc approach and put
systems in place that will stay the course
– modular containers, for example, that
can be added to as need arises.

Containers
Sturdy, portable plastic boxes or
wicker baskets are ideal for storing
toys. Keep like with like for easy
retrieval. Shelve them low down
for easy access or build in a low
display shelf and store containers
underneath. Desirable items kept
on upper levels only encourage
children to climb in search of them.

Clothes storage
Most of the items of clothing small
children possess are foldable, so
a simple chest of drawers can be
used to house the bulk of their
wardrobe, along with toiletries
and bed linen. As the child grows,
hanging space will also be
required. Built-in closets look
neater than freestanding pieces.

Peg rails and racks
A low peg rail or rack is a useful
way of organizing aprons, cloth
bags of games kit and swimming
gear, and outdoor clothes –
anything that is in regular use.
A rail or rack for each child
reinforces the sense of ownership
and cuts down on squabbles.

Left — A teenager's room needs to be versatile. Moving the bed up a level can be a good way of providing more storage or working space underneath, while keeping the floor clear for relaxing and lounging about.

Below — Wardrobes (closets) built into the alcoves on either side of a redundant chimney breast provide capacious places to store clothing and accessories. Narrow shelving painted hot pink serves as a controlled display area.

Teenage

Many running battles that break out between teenagers and their parents centre on possessions – how and where they are kept. While tidiness is not high on the list of priorities of this age group, you can at least help them on their way to better habits by providing good systems of organization. Whether these are put to use is up to them – you can always close the door on the mess.

Wall space

Extensive shelving, preferably built-in, will take care of most storage needs – books, school files, DVDs and CDs – and will go some way to addressing the teenager's tendency to use the floor as a dumping ground. Shelving can incorporate a wider surface or a pull-out or pull-down desk.

Display areas

Few teenagers can resist the temptation to collage every surface with posters and memorabilia – it is how they experiment with style at a time of life when notions of identity are fluid and developing. To protect the paintwork, you can always line the wall with cork to make a large-scale display area.

Platform beds

One way of gaining more space in a teenager's room that is on the small side is to move the bed up a level. The area underneath can then be used either as a study space or den, or to accommodate built-in clothes storage.

Out-of-the-way storage

Make use of out-of-the-way areas for the bulkier items of teenage kit, such as sports equipment and outdoor gear.

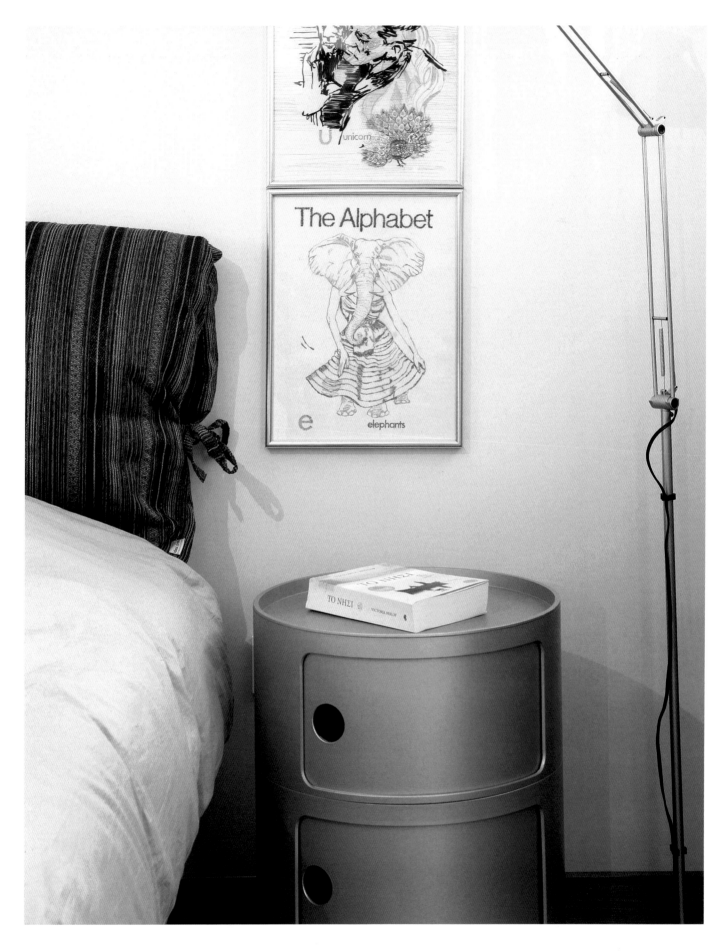

COMPONIBILI
STORAGE SYSTEM

Architect and designer Anna Castelli Ferrieri (1920–2006) was a leading light in post-war Italian design. Together with her husband, Giulio Castelli, she founded Kartell, the Milanese manufacturer that has done so much to enhance the image of plastic as a desirable consumer material. The Componibili storage system, which she designed in 1969, has been a great success ever since it was launched. In 1972, when the exhibition 'Italy: The New Domestic Landscape' opened at the Museum of Modern Art in New York, Bloomingdale's home furnishings department featured an entire New York skyline created out of stacked Componibili units.

The system is available either as modular units that stack together or as fixed two- or three-tiered stand-alone pieces, and in square or round formats. The modular units stack in any configuration and require only one lid per tower. Made of injection-moulded ABS plastic (ABS is a type of thermoplastic), the system comes in a variety of colours.

Cheerful, functional and versatile, the Componibili slots into many different areas of the home – as side tables in bedrooms and as occasional storage in kitchens, bathrooms and home offices. Children particularly enjoy stowing their belongings behind the curved sliding doors.

PLAIN

SIMPLE

USEFUL

----

bathing

Left — A vanity unit
suspended from the wall
provides space for double
sinks, along with concealed
storage behind flush panels
secured with press catches.
Neatness of detailing is
crucial in fitted rooms.

Generous tiling extends
from floor to ceiling. The
taps (faucets) are mounted
directly on the mirror.
Underfloor heating makes
the bathroom a pleasant
place to be, whatever the
weather outside.

bathing

Simplicity is nowhere more welcome than in the surroundings where we perform that most elemental of all activities: bathing. Bathing is only partly about personal hygiene and getting clean; it is also a time for relaxation, daydreaming and letting stresses and strains wash away. For children young enough to share a bath, it is another kind of playtime. Whether it is an invigorating shower at the start of the day or a long, hot soak at the end of it, nothing should get in the way of this most basic of all pleasures.

Yet the plain, simple and useful approach should not be misinterpreted as a return to those Spartan, somewhat punitive arrangements that characterized 'the smallest room' for many decades. Rather it means a layout that makes optimum use of space, fixtures and fittings that work properly, and surfaces and finishes that are easy to keep in sparkling condition. It also means paying attention to detail and accessories: nothing beats really thick, absorbent bath towels warmed on a heated rail, or a properly lit mirror for shaving or putting on makeup.

LAYOUTS

Bathrooms, shower rooms and cloakrooms (guest washrooms) are the most tightly planned and fitted areas in the home, even more so than kitchens. Like kitchens, layout will be largely determined by existing servicing arrangements; unlike kitchens, space is often in short supply.

This puts the onus on thorough planning right from the outset. A few millimetres here and there can make all the difference between a layout that works and one that falls short. Consult a professional or use an in-house design service to avoid making mistakes that will be costly and disruptive to rectify.

○ Site bathing areas as close to the bedroom as possible.
○ If you have plenty of space to play with, consider a more dynamic arrangement, with the tub placed centrally or projecting out at right angles from the wall.
○ Arrange the bathroom layout so that the toilet is screened in some way from the bathtub, or at least so that it doesn't align with the head of the tub.

○ Wall-hung fixtures such as toilets and sinks can be neatly integrated with built-in storage so that cistern, soil pipe and plumbing runs are concealed.
○ Tubs and showers must have sufficient surrounding space to make access easy and safe. Similarly, you will need enough elbow room to either side of the sink.
○ The diagram below shows typical clearances for bathroom fixtures – the optimum distances needed for easy access.

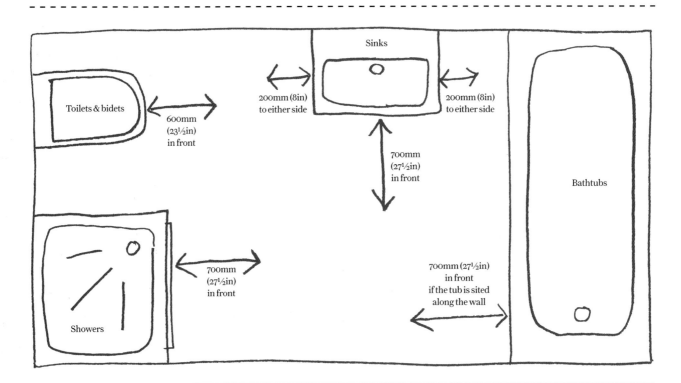

Toilets & bidets — 600mm (23½in) in front

Sinks — 200mm (8in) to either side — 200mm (8in) to either side — 700mm (27½in) in front

Showers — 700mm (27½in) in front

Bathtubs — 700mm (27½in) in front if the tub is sited along the wall

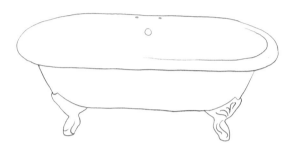

CAST-IRON
BATHTUB

First produced in the late nineteenth century, the cast-iron bathtub has a certain timeless quality that makes it equally at home in contemporary interiors as it is in more traditional settings. The interior of the bathtub is vitreous enamel; the process of enamelling cast-iron was developed by Scottish-born American inventor David Dunbar Buick (1854–1929), more famous for founding the car company of the same name.

Cast-iron tubs, with their scrolled roll tops, are freestanding features that can be placed centrally in a bathroom, at right angles to a wall or aligned with it. The typical accompaniment is decorative claw feet; shaped wooden rests have a cleaner, more modern appeal. The exterior of the bathtub can be painted to blend in with a decorative scheme.

Compared to a steel tub, a cast-iron tub is much more durable. Because it is completely rigid and doesn't flex under weight, the finish is less at risk from cracking and the tub is, therefore, much more rust-resistant. It also maintains heat for longer and its generous size makes it ideal for long, leisurely soaks.

FAMILY BATHROOMS

Multi-use and multi-generational,
family bathrooms work best where
space is generous. This means you can
allow extra room around the tub for
helping out at bath-time when children
are small. It also gives you the option of
installing twin sinks, which helps keep
harmony when everyone is trying to get
ready at the start of the day. A separate
shower cubicle adds to the versatility.

○ All surfaces and finishes must
be fully waterproof – children's
bath-times tend to be splashy
affairs. Be generous with wall
tiling and use moisture-resistant
paint on the walls. Ensure floors
are as nonslip as possible. Tiling
or stone flooring with a slight
texture are better options than
those that are perfectly smooth.

○ Take the opportunity, if
possible, to site laundry facilities
– the washing machine and
dryer – either in the bathroom
or a short distance away from it.

○ Provide adequate storage for
the necessities and accessories of
each family member, in separate
holders or containers so everyone
knows whose is whose.

○ Vivid colour accents can be
provided by those details that
are easy to change: bathmats
and towels, bath toys and
storage containers.

○ Frameless shower doors and enclosures have a neater, more minimal look.

SHOWERS AND WET ROOMS

While bathtubs provide the opportunity for long, contemplative soaks, showers are brisk, invigorating wake-up calls or instant refreshers. A shower 'room' can be nothing more elaborate than a screened or curtained enclosure at the head of the bathtub; at its most extensive and inclusive, it shades into the wet room, where the 'cubicle' is formed by the walls of the room itself and water drains directly to the floor. Midway between the two is the shower cubicle, which is available in various configurations.

○ Shower heads vary enormously in size, material, shape and type of spray. While your choice will be governed by performance, aesthetics shouldn't take a back seat – some are more sculptural than others.

○ Ceramic shower trays are better than acrylic or enamelled steel because they are stronger and more stable.

○ Shower controls range from the standard bath-shower mixer to highly sophisticated thermostatic controls. Look out for designs that are easy to operate and that maintain a reliable temperature. Mixers often don't.

○ A wet room, the ultimate in back-to-basics bathing, is a particularly good solution if the space at your disposal is small or awkwardly shaped. Full waterproofing of all surfaces is essential and dense materials must be used as cladding, which increases the load on the floor.

Left — A freestanding tub placed in the centre of the room is complemented by the simple and equally sculptural floor-mounted tap (faucet) – the perfect setting for relaxing soaks.

Below — When choosing bathroom fixtures and fittings, coordination is the order of the day. Mixing and matching styles, materials and colours is visually jolting in a room that is often on the small side and where the layout is fixed. Make sure you allow enough space around each fixture for easy access.

CHOOSING FIXTURES

Compared to only a decade or so ago, bathroom fixtures are now available in a huge selection of materials, shapes and sizes. Focusing on simplicity – of maintenance as well as form – helps to narrow the bewildering array of choice. Wooden bathtubs and glass sinks, for example, might have a certain cachet, but they are more demanding in upkeep.

○ While a bathtub can display an aesthetic of its own, it is best to coordinate the design of other fixtures – sink, toilet and bidet – for a coherent effect. Durable vitreous china remains by far the most prevalent material.

○ Avoid coloured bathroom suites. Classic white is best: it doesn't date, it is practical and space-enhancing, and items of sanitaryware can be replaced at a subsequent time without worrying about colour-matching.

○ Sinks in the form of simple circular or rectangular vessels that are mounted directly on top of vanity units have a pleasing sculptural quality.

○ Tubs should be comfortable: both long enough and deep enough to fit your frame. Sinks should be able to hold a sufficient volume of water to suit the uses to which you will put them – for example, a small corner sink will do for a cloakroom (guest washroom) but will be inadequate elsewhere. Toilets and bidets need to be fixed at the right height for you.

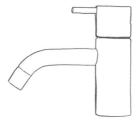

VOLA

MIXER

This classic range of taps (faucets) was first designed in 1968 by the famous Danish architect Arne Jacobsen (1902–71) as part of his last commission, the Danish National Bank in Copenhagen. Jacobsen rarely designed furniture or fittings outside of the context in which they were intended to be used. Known for his control of detail, his ambition was to create fully integrated spaces. The design for the tap (faucet) was the result of a collaboration between Jacobsen and Verner Overgaard. Overgaard, the owner of Vola, a manufacturing company that was dedicated to innovation, approached Jacobsen after he won the competition to design the bank. The overall concept was to produce a wall-mounted fixture where the mechanical parts are concealed, with only the handle and spout visible, as if the tap (faucet) were a continuation of a water pipe. The sculptural, timeless result won immediate international acclaim and has been in production ever since. Over the years, other designs have been added to the range and a number of technical specifications have been altered, but the essential aesthetic remains unchanged.

Below — Small bulbs along the top edge of a bathroom mirror – reminiscent of the lighting arrangements in theatrical dressing rooms – light the face evenly.

Right — All bathrooms need more than one source of artificial lighting. A single bright overhead fixture deadens the atmosphere and can be somewhat punitive in effect. Here recessed downlights supply background light, while a light fitting concealed under the mirrored cabinet illuminates the sink.

LIGHTING

People often make the mistake of assuming that a bathroom needs only general background light – hence the depressing ubiquity of the single overhead fixture. In fact, all bathrooms, no matter how small, benefit from more than one light source, for mood and atmosphere as much as for carrying out daily ablutions. Natural light is a bonus; so, too, is a view. However, unlike other 'habitable' rooms or living areas, there is no legal requirement for a bathroom to have a window.

○ Safety is a key consideration. All light fittings should be specifically designed for bathroom use and fully enclosed in a waterproof casing. The type and positioning of switches must comply with regulations.

○ Recessed downlights are ideal for bathrooms. Because the layout is fixed, you can position them to target light at specific areas, knowing that the arrangement will not change at some future date. Fully enclosed wall lights are another option.

○ Put bathroom lighting on dimmer controls to vary the mood.

○ Mirrors that are lit either all the way around the perimeter or to both sides will give the most pleasing reflection, as the light falls evenly onto the face. Toplighting, on the other hand, casts harsh, unflattering shadows. Some bathroom mirrors have integral lighting.

Left — We are more acutely
aware of the varying qualities
of surfaces and finishes in the
bathroom because our bare
skin comes in direct contact
with them. A neutral-toned
scatter rug provides an
element of comfort on the
concrete floor; better still
is underfloor heating.

Below — Sleek stainless-steel
taps (faucets), hand-held
sprays and controls have
a sculptural presence.

SURFACES AND FINISHES

The bottom line of bathroom décor is
that it must be fully waterproof in those
locations where it needs to be and
water-resistant everywhere else. This
means the surfaces that are liable to be
splashed – around bathtubs, showers
and sinks – need to be clad in some
impervious or sealed material. Other
finishes should be wipeable, at least
– paints designated for bathroom use,
for example, contain vinyl, which
withstands the effect of condensation.
Special attention should also be paid
to seals and joints. Similarly, flooring
materials that provide a little grip
underfoot are better than those that
become lethally slippery when wet.

All-white or pale-toned bathrooms
have a pure, refreshing simplicity,
particularly if there is a good quality
of natural light. But because bathrooms
are self-contained areas that we chiefly
experience behind closed doors, strong
colour can play a role. Deep, moody
blues, for example, are restful and
contemplative, with appropriately
watery connotations. Brighter, warmer
shades of yellow and red, which might
be too intense in living areas or large
doses, can be uplifting in cloakrooms
(guest washrooms) where we don't
linger for long.

Below — Yellow strikes a sunny, uplifting note. You can afford to be bold with colour when it is restricted to a small, enclosed area where you are less likely to tire of it sooner rather than later.

Below right — Water-resistant, anti-slip and with a pleasing textural character, tiling is a versatile and practical bathroom finish. The scale of the tile, as much as colour and material, will dictate the overall effect.

○ Because surface areas in bathrooms tend to be relatively limited, you might be able to afford to use more expensive materials than you would otherwise have chosen.

○ Woods such as cedar and teak are naturally water-resistant and can even be used as the bases for showers. Hardwood floors should be sealed and laid over marine ply to prevent warping. Yacht varnish is the best protective coating for softwood flooring. But wood, solid or veneered, is perhaps most versatile in the form of vanity tops and cabinetry, where it contributes textural variety and depth of character.

○ Stone has a timeless, classic beauty. It is available in a variety of thicknesses and formats for use on walls, floors or vanity tops. Cool limestone has a contemporary elegance, while dark, moody slate adds graphic impact.

○ Tiling is a ubiquitous bathroom finish, for splashbacks, shower stalls and underfoot. Ring the changes with larger, bevelled formats or opt for mosaic, which provides a good grip underfoot and is an excellent way of delivering luminous colour.

○ Linoleum, particularly in sheet form, makes a supremely practical and attractive bathroom floor. Unlike vinyl, which is synthetic and does not improve with use, lino is natural, ages well and is anti-bacterial. Colours are soft and mottled. Another option is studded rubber, which is nonslip and comes in a choice of vibrant shades.

○ Toughened and laminated glass is ideal for shower enclosures, partitions, sink or tub splashbacks and vanity tops.

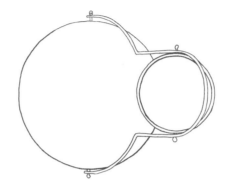

ORBIT

MIRROR

Mirrors may be an indispensable bathroom feature, but most mass-market products lack the charm and finesse of the Orbit (1984), designed by British designer Rodney Kinsman (b. 1943) and produced by the Italian company Bieffe. Kinsman, founder and director of OMK, had a long association with Habitat in its early days, and has since become well known for the design of public seating.

As the name suggests, the design consists of a large fixed circular mirror, with a smaller orbiting satellite. One side of the smaller mirror is a magnifier. In other words, you get three mirrors in one – useful for seeing side and rear reflections, as well as closer detail for shaving and applying makeup.

The Orbit is made of tubular steel finished with polished chrome or oven-baked epoxy. The large mirror is attached to the wall using a simple keyhole slot. The smaller mirror rotates through 180 degrees and swivels on its own axis. The use of material and engineering precision recalls early modernist design, and the mobility of the mirror gives it an animating quality.

Left — Most bathrooms need a combination of concealed and open storage. The former is ideal for bulk supplies, spare bath linen and products you don't want on display.

Open shelving or ledges near sinks and bathtubs can be used as places to keep bathing and beauty products that are in daily use.

Below — A wall-mounted mirrored cabinet provides discreet stowing space for bathroom products, keeping the vanity top clear.

STORAGE AND DISPLAY

There is a fine line between keeping the lotions and potions you use every day close at hand and cluttering up every surface with a skyline of grooming aids. Incorporate concealed storage, such as vanity units and cupboards built in behind dummy walls, at the same time as you plan the layout of the bathroom fixtures for a neat and well-integrated approach that provides enough room to house essentials. Storage tackled afterwards can look piecemeal.

○ Open shelving is a practical solution for products and accessories that are in regular use or items that you need to keep at arm's reach – spare towels, for example. Glass shelves are easy to clean and do not stain or discolour like wood.

○ Heated rails are a good way of organizing towels and may deliver enough space-heating for a small bathroom or shower room. Mobile trolleys are another option.

○ Decant products into an array of lidded containers or glass jars for a more considered look.

○ Soap and toothbrushes need to drain – soap in a wire rack or perforated or ridged dish and toothbrushes in a wall-mounted holder or similar.

○ Wall cabinets with a mirrored front, shaving point and integral lighting offer versatile storage space, but may not be the best places to keep medicines that require cooler conditions.

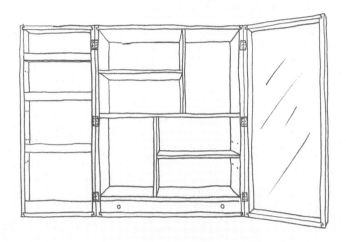

BATHROOM CUPBOARD

The third and final variation on my storage cupboard is this bathroom cabinet. Wall-hung storage makes especially good sense in the bathroom, where floor area is often limited. Similarly, both for reasons of space and to provide a relaxing environment that is free of visual clutter, discreet behind-the-scenes storage is a positive advantage – while many lotions and potions come in forms of packaging that are attractive enough to display, you don't want to crowd every available surface with an untidy skyline of jars and bottles.

Like the others in the series, this cupboard is made of wood, which gives great depth of character and has a pleasing tactility. A significant design departure is the mirror attached to the back of one of the hinged panels. Narrow shelves lining the other panel hold a collection of bathing and beauty products. The main body of the cupboard is subdivided into a number of compartments of varying heights and widths to accommodate different sizes and shapes of possessions. A shallow drawer at the base provides a place to store razors, tweezers and other grooming aids. The door should be lockable to keep children away from any medicine. Full step-by-step instructions on how to make the cupboard can be viewed online at www.octopusbooks.co.uk/psu.

STOCKISTS

Featured design icons

For stockists in your area, see manufacturer's website.

Mauviel Copper Cookware
www.mauviel.com

Kilner Jar
www.kilnerjar.co.uk

Moka Espresso Pot
www.bialetti.it

Le Creuset Casserole
www.lecreuset.com

Wishbone Chair
www.carlhansen.com

Duralex Glassware
www.duralex.com

Karuselli Chair
www.avarte-cn.com

Glo-Ball F3 Light
www.flos.com

**Anglepoise®
Original1227™ Light**
www.anglepoise.com

Leonardo Trestle Table
www.zanotta.it

**606 Universal
Shelving System**
www.vitsoe.com

The Duvet
- see *Furniture & furnishings*

Snow Chest of Drawers
www.asplund.org

**Componibili
Storage System**
www.kartell.it

Cast-iron Bath
- See *Kitchens & bathrooms*

Conran products & collections

JCPenney
**Design by Conran
exclusively for JCPenney**
www.jcpenney.com

Page 77 from the
Spring 2013 collection.

Page 98–99 from the
Spring 2013 collection.

Conran M&S
www.marksandspencer.
com/Conran

Page 57 from the
Autumn 2012 collection.

The Conran Shop
www.conran.com

Special projects

All three special projects
included in this book were
made by Michael Howard
and built at Benchmark, our
furniture-making business.
www.benchmarkfurniture.com
For full instructions on how
to make the cupboards
yourself, go to www.
octopusbooks.co.uk/psu.

Furniture & furnishings

Classic contemporary
furniture and one-stop stores.

Aram
www.aram.co.uk

B&B Italia
www.bebitalia.it

Crate & Barrel
www.crateandbarrel.com

Habitat
www.habitat.net

Home Depot
www.homedepot.com

Ikea
www.ikea.co.uk
www.ikea.com

John Lewis
www.johnlewis.com

Knoll International
www.knoll.com

Muji
www.muji.com

Pottery Barn
www.potterybarn.com

SCP
www.scp.co.uk

Skandium
www.skandium.com

Twentytwentyone
www.twentytwentyone.com

Kitchens & bathrooms

Agape
www.agapedesign.it

Alternative Plans
www.alternativebathrooms.
com

Armitage-Shanks
www.armitage-shanks.co.uk

Aston Matthews
www.astonmatthews.co.uk

**Avante Bathroom
Products**
www.avantebathrooms.com

Bathstore
www.bathstore.com

Bed Bath and Beyond
www.bedbathandbeyond.
com

Boffi
www.boffi.com

Bulthaup
www.bulthaup.com

Dornbracht
www.dornbracht.com

Ideal Standard
www.ideal-standard.co.uk

Plain English
www.plainenglishdesign.
co.uk

Siematic
www.siematic.com

Villeroy & Boch
www.villeroy-boch.com

PICTURE ACKNOWLEDGEMENTS

The publisher would like to thank the following photographers, agencies, companies and architects for their kind permission to reproduce the photographs in this book:

2 Getty Images; 6 Stephan Julliard/Tripod Agency; 8–9 Richard Powers (Architects: Knut Hjeltnes); 16 Hans Mossel/Pure Public (Styling: Sabine Burkunk); 18–19 Jake Curtis/Media 10 Images; 24 Birgitta W. Drejer/Sisters Agency (Stylist: Pernille Vest); 25 Mark Luscombe-Whyte/Homes & Gardens/IPC+ Syndication; 26–27 Petra Bindel/House of Pictures (Styling: Emma Persson Lagerberg/House of Pictures); 29 James Merrell/Living Etc/IPC+ Syndication; 30–31 Ben Anders; 32 Hans Zeegers/Taverne Agency; 34 James Merrell/Livingetc/IPC+ Syndication; 35 Richard Powers/Livingetc/IPC+ Syndication; 36 Birgitta W. Drejer/Sisters Agency (Architects: Emil Humbert and Christophe Poyet) www.humbertpoyet.com; 37 Prue Ruscoe/Taverne Agency; 38 Eric d'Herouville/Maison Magazine (Designer: Marie-Maud Levron); 39 Patric Johansson; 40 Anna Kern/House of Pictures (Styling: Linda Åhman/House of Pictures); 41 Ray Main/Mainstream Images; 42 Alessandra Ianniello/HomeStories; 44 left James Balston/Arcaid (Architect: Gianni Botsford); 44 right Daniella Witte; 45 left Dana van Leeuwen/Taverne Agency; 45 right Anouk de Kleermaeker/Taverne Agency; 48 Jake Curtis/Livingetc/IPC+ Syndication; 49 Julian Cornish-Trestrail/Media 10 Images; 50 Mikkel Vang/Taverne Agency; 52 Paul Massey/Livingetc/IPC+ Syndication; 53 Mark Bolton/GAP Interiors; 54 Andreas von Einsiedel; 55 Jake Curtis/IPC+ Syndication; 56 Greg Cox/Bureaux/GAP Interiors; 57 Debi Treloar (Catalogue: Conran M&S Autumn 2012); 58 Verity Welstead/Narratives; 60 and 62 Guy Obijn (Interior architect: Kaaidesign, Antwerp, Belgium); 64 Jean-Marc Palisse/Cote Paris (Architect: Thomas Fourtane); 65 above Prue Ruscoe/Taverne Agency; 65 below Birgitta W. Drejer/Sisters Agency (Stylist: Pernille Vest; Owner: Barbara Hvidt from Soft Gallery); 66 Chris Tubbs/Media 10 Images; 68–69 Mirjam Bleeker (Architects: Doepel Strijkers); 70 Paul Massey/Livingetc/IPC+ Syndication; 72 Tara Pearce; 74 Ben Anders (Owner: Bianca Hall of Kiss Her); 75 Mikkel Mortensen (Stylist: Gitte Kjaer); 76 Ben Anders (Architects: Huttunen Lipasti Pakkanen); 77 Design By Conran Exclusively for JCPenney; 78–79 Alessandra Ianniello/HomeStories; 80 Kira Brandt/Pure Public (Stylist: Glotti); 81 David Prince/Red Cover/Photoshot; 82 Kira Brandt/Pure Public (Stylist: Katrine Martensen-Larsen); 83 Birgitta W. Drejer/Sisters Agency (Owner: fashion designer, Charlotte Vadum); 84 Birgitta W. Drejer/Sisters Agency; 85 Martin Cederblad (Stylist: Charlotte Pettersson); 87 Brigitte Kroone/House of Pictures; 90 Jody Stewart/Homes & Gardens/IPC+ Syndication; 91 Catherine Gratwicke/Homes & Gardens/IPC+ Syndication; 98–99 Design By Conran Exclusively for JCPenney; 100 Brigitta W. Drejer/Sisters Agency (Stylist: Pernille Vest; Owner: Design Unit); 101 Ioana Marinescu (Architect: David Kohn); 102 Paul Massey/Livingetc/IPC+ Syndication; 106 Mark Williams/Red Cover/Photoshot; 107 Simon Upton/The Interior Archive (Architect: John Pawson); 112 Line Klein; 113 Jefferson Smith/Media 10 Images; 114 Mikkel Adsbøl/Pure Public (Katrine Martensen-Larsen); 115 Bart van Leuven (Interior Architect: Jean-Pierre Detaeye); 118 Birgitta W. Drejer/Sisters Agency (Sylist: Pernille Vest; Owner: fashion designer, Malene Birger); 119 Tria Giovan/GAP Interiors; 122 Max Zambelli; 123 Ben Anders/Media 10 Images (Cabinet: Russell Pinch); 124 Fabio Lombrici/Red Cover/Photoshot; 126 Mikko Ryhänen, courtesy of Artek; 132 Mark Williams/Red Cover/Photoshot; 133 Costas Picadas/GAP Interiors; 134 Martin Gardner (Stylist: Emma Hooton)/courtesy of Anglepoise; 136 Max Zambelli; 137 Costas Picadas/GAP Interiors; 138 James Merrell/Livingetc/IPC+ Syndication; 139 Simon Upton/The Interior Archive (Designer: Michael Gabellini); 140–141 Gaelle Le Boulicaut; 142 Jonas Bjerre-Poulsen/Norm Architects; 143 Martin Hahn & Shelly Street/Narratives; 147 Bieke Claessens/GAP Interiors; 148 left Electrolux; 148 right Polly Wreford/Homes & Gardens/IPC+ Syndication; 149 left Nathalie Krag/Taverne Agency; 149 right Paul Massey/Red Cover/Photoshot; 150 Thomas Stewart/Media 10 Images; 152 Sarah Blee (Architect: Claudio Silvestrin); 160 C.Dugied/MCM/Camera Press (Owner: Painter, Catherine Lê-Van); 161 Frédéric Vasseur/MCM/Camera Press; 162–163 Chris Tubbs/Media 10 Images; 164 Dana van Leeuwen/Taverne Agency; 165 Earl Carter/Taverne Agency; 168 Greg Cox/H&L/GAP Interiors (Styling: Jeanne Botes); 169 Karel Balas/Milk/Vega mg; 170 Marjon Hoogervorst/Taverne Agency; 172 Bieke Claessens/GAP Interiors; 173 Andreas von Einsiedel/View; 174 left Jean-Marc Palisse/Cote Paris (Architect: Mathurin Hardel, Cyril Le Bihan); 174 right Andreas von Einsiedel; 175 Simon Griffiths/Bauer Media Group/Camera Press; 176 Pernilla Hed (Styling: Daniel Bergman); 178 Jake Curtis/Livingetc/IPC Syndication; 180 Dana van Leeuwen/Taverne Agency; 181 Earl Carter/Taverne Agency; 182 James Merrell/Livingetc/IPC+ Syndication; 183 Jake Fitzjones/GAP Interiors (Charlotte Crosland Interiors); 184 Costas Picadas/GAP Interiors; 191 Rachel Whiting/GAP Interiors; 192 Tim Evan-Cook/Livingetc/IPC+ Syndication; 193 Greg Cox/H&L/GAP Interiors (Styling: Kate Boswell); 194 Andreas von Einsiedel; 196 Luke White/The Interior Archive (Architect: Sandra Kesselring); 197 Jake Curtis/Livingetc/IPC Syndication; 198 Birgitta W. Drejer/Sisters Agency (Owner: Charlotte Lynggaard); 199 Chris Tubbs/Media 10 Images; 202 Serge Brison/Hemis/Camera Press; 203 Brent Darby/Narratives; 204 Jonas Bjerre-Poulsen/Norm Architects; 206 Ben Anders/Homes & Gardens/IPC+ Syndication; 207 Gaelle Le Boulicaut; 208 Birgitta W. Drejer/Sisters Agency; 210 left Ben Anders (Architects: Studiomama); 210 right John Paul Urizar/Bauer Media Group/Camera Press; 211 left Alessandra Ianniello/HomeStories; 211 right Greg Cox/Bureaux/GAP Interiors (Styling: Sven Alberding); 212 Andreas von Einsiedel (Architect: John Minshaw); 214 Inigo Bujedo Aguirre/View.

Every effort has been made to trace the copyright holders. We apologize in advance for any unintentional omissions and would be pleased to insert the appropriate acknowledgement in any subsequent edition.

The following photographs were taken specially for Conran Octopus by: Paul Raeside 4–5; 10; 12; 20; 22; 46–47; 86; 88;94; 96; 104–105; 116–117; 128; 130; 146; 156; 158; 186; 188; 200–201; 209. Nick Pope 15; 28; 92; 108; 110; 144; 154; 167.

INDEX

First published in 2014 by Conran Octopus Ltd
a part of Octopus Publishing Group
Endeavour House, 189 Shaftesbury Avenue,
London WC2H 8JY
www.octopusbooks.co.uk

An Hachette UK Company
www.hachette.co.uk

Distributed in the US by
Hachette Book Group USA
237 Park Avenue, New York, NY 10017 USA

Distributed in Canada by
Canadian Manda Group
165 Dufferin Street, Toronto, Ontario,
Canada M6K 3H6

British Library Cataloguing-in-Publication Data.
A catalogue record for this book is available from
the British Library.

ISBN 978 1 84091 655 3
Printed in China

Contributing Editor: Elizabeth Wilhide
Publisher: Alison Starling
Design & Art Direction: Jonathan Christie
Senior Editor: Sybella Stephens
Copy Editor: Zia Mattocks
Picture Researcher: Liz Boyd
Senior Production Manager: Katherine Hockley